CW00807217

# EXPENDABLE

## THOMAS COTTER

### EDITED BY LILLIAN KING

WINDFALL BOOKS

ISBN NO: 0 9539839 4 3

*Expendable*

# ACKNOWLEDGEMENTS

I would like to thank my daughter and three sons for their help in the land of computers, and my long suffering wife Ruth, for her patience and understanding during the period when this story was being formed.

Edited by Lillian King
Cover design by Ray Cotter
Printed by A4 Print Dunfermline

Typesetting, layout and design by Windfall Books
Published by Windfall Books
2 Railway Cottages
Westcroft Way
Kelty KY4 0AT

# ABOUT THE AUTHOR

Thomas Cotter was, among other things, a local Scoutmaster in Valleyfield, a Home Office Instructor on Civil Defence during the Cuban crisis, and a policeman in Rosyth Dockyard. He also saw action with the RAF during World War II. All of his working life, however, from 1939 till he was made redundant in 1986, was spent in the mining industry. Forty six years service in the mines was not exceptional. Many miners did as much and more. In his father's day men didn't retire, they worked until they died. Tom's experiences led him to believe that men were expendable, both in the air and underground in the mines.

He now lives in Spain. His hobbies are astronomy, golf and gardening.

# FOREWORD

## by Councillor William Clarke JP

I am delighted to be given the opportunity to write the foreword for a book that describes life in the coal mines and in the communities where the miners and their families lived.

Born and reared in the village of Glencraig, Tom Cotter was a product of his time, experiencing at first hand the tremendous spirit that gave the community and the people who lived with in it a heart. People had little material wealth but they lived by a common bond that made them honest, fiercely independent and proud. Miners wages were poor, their working conditions dangerous and terrible, and many paid with their lives the price of producing coal. Although there were various disasters in Scotland, Fife unfortunately had more than its share.

Tom points to Donibristle, Bowhill, Lindsay, Valleyfield, Michael and Seafield as illustrations of the dangers involved. Press headlines praised the miners for their courage but campaigned against them as greedy when they fought for decent wages.

On a more lighthearted note, Tom describes the various pastimes - pigeons, hens, ducks, gardening, fishing, shooting, bowling, boxing and, of course, pitch and toss. Miners tended to be gamblers and 'tossing schools' were common. Sometimes in extreme cases men lost all their wages but most miners gambled only what they could afford, and though no-one would defend it, money was of little importance compared to men gambling with their lives underground every day.

In the book, Tom writes about the dancing at the local Miners Welfare, where a great many romances commenced and blossomed into marriage. Dance night and balls were highlights in every mining community. The miners paid for their own culture. Contributions from their wages were deducted for everything from local pipe and silver bands, football teams, galas and Miners Welfares. When anything financial was required, the miners were never found wanting.

The importance of women in mining communities has, in my opinion, never been recognised. Until nationalisation in 1947, many girls left

*Expendable*

school at the age of fourteen and went straight to work at the pithead. Indeed the last women to work on the pithead in Scotland were working at the Minto Colliery till its close in 1967. If miners were slaves their women were slaves to slaves. They had to rear large families, with men on different shifts, and no washing machines or hoovers. They sacrificed themselves for their families every day of every year. Because of the harshness of their lives, many died young or were old before their time.

We are indebted to Tom, who has taken time and devoted energy to produce a book which describes the times when over a million men were employed in the coal industry. It is vital to record at both local and national level the contribution of miner, their wives and families, to this nation. This debt has still to be repaid.

In this book, Tom brings alive people and incidents long past. I sincerely hope that younger readers are inspired by these factual accounts and that those who lived and worked during these times will take some pride in this book.

Finally, many thanks to Tom Cotter, for this labour of love.

*Willie Clarke November 2003*

# CONTENTS

Chapter One- Ghost Section                1

Chapter Two –Glencraig                11

Chapter Three – A Miner's Life          24

Chapter Four – Pan Engine Boy          35

Chapter Five –Wee, Sleekit, Cow'ring Tim,rous Beastie    45

Chapter Six – A Near Thing             56

Chapter Seven – Jenny Gray            64

Chapter Eight – Coal At a Price          77

Chapter Nine – Laurence Dailey         95

Chapter Ten – Strike                   104

Chapter Eleven –Embarrassing Moments     116

Chapter Twelve –Nightmare            130

Chapter Thirteen – Playtime            141

Chapter Fourteen – Rescue Brigade      146

Chapter Fifteen – Trials and Tribulations    151

Chapter Sixteen –Travel Tours Underground   160

Chapter Seventeen – Finale            166

Glossary                      170

# CHAPTER ONE

## GHOST SECTION

It was a Friday, night shift, I remember that, but I don't remember the exact date. George Morrison, Rab Gray, my brother Maurice and I were part of a team of stone miners, and at that time we were working at the Aitken Colliery near the town of Kelty. We all came from the village of Glencraig, except Rab, who was from Lochore. Leaving the house for work we would cut across the fields, cross the burn, then over the Clune Hill to the pit, into the pit head baths, change to working clothes and assemble on the pit head where we would all go down the pit together.

That Friday night, only three of us turned up - Wee Geordie, as we knew him, Rab and I. My brother Maurice, who had hurt his back earlier in the week, was forced to stay at home. He never lost a shift unless there was something badly wrong; none of us did, not with the wages we were getting.

Arriving at our place of work, we hung our jackets on a nail and sat down to eat a slice of bread, which we always did, before starting to work. Wee Geordie was the leading man and he would set the pace. When he got to his feet, adjusting his belt, we stood up too.

"We'll make a start," he said, "the oversman can't give us a replacement for Maurice. Absenteeism is high tonight, he says."

Rab, always the jovial type, got to his feet and fixed his lamp on his head.

"What does he expect? It's Friday, pay day, they'll all be in the pub. That's where we should be if we had any sense."

"You haven't," laughed Wee Geordie. "That's why you are here."

Wee Geordie was small, but he was built like a horse, with shoulders of a man twice his height, calm, quiet, but for all he spoke quietly there was authority in his voice. He'd been in mining all his life and must have been around fifty. I can remember he always chewed tobacco even in the even in the pub. He'd put his chew to one side of his mouth whilst drinking a pint of beer. On Friday he'd bring a sponge cake to the pit to share with us, and break it apart with his hands always managing to keep the biggest bit for himself. Once I said to him that it wasn't polite to keep the big bit to him self. He looked up at me with raised eyebrows.

"Well, what would you do then?" he asked

"I would offer you the large piece and keep the small bit."

"Well that's exactly what I did, I've got the big bit," he said.

That was Wee Geordie, always had an answer, I suppose that's why I admired him. Rab was much the same type of a man. That's why they got on so well at work. Rab would joke and laugh a lot and generally took things in his stride, but there the similarity ended.

Rab, a tall, slim, muscular, strong man, always had a ragged unkempt appearance. He never took his pit clothes home to be mended and his trousers were almost in tatters. His excuse was that if he took them home to his wife she'd hit him with them. At the end of his shift whilst undoing his boots, he'd complain was that someone had tied his laces into knots again.

Maurice fitted in well with those two. Me, I was not long out of the Royal Air Force, where I was a member of a bombing crew and was only feeling my way and getting back to where I left off.

Before we got started to work, we saw a light approaching. It was the oversman's headlamp.

"I need your team Geordie, I've a couple of packers short in No. 5 Section. The Deputy is waiting on you. Oh, and take your graith."

Then he was off.

"Christ," Rab said, "You know what that means - the roof's ready for a close, that's why they've stayed at home. Like I said, it's the pub I should be in, along with the packers."

I wasn't that green behind the ears not to know what he meant. No. 5 had a thick post roof of sandstone and when the coal was removed from beneath it, it would break up and collapse, taking the weight off the face and providing rubble to build packs. Good packs have a stabilising effect on the roof but with no rubble to build with it could be very dangerous. The packers who worked there knew the mood of the roof and could tell when a close was near and didn't want to be there when it happened.

"You could be right, Rab," Wee Geordie agreed.

I was thinking that if it was bad for the packers it didn't look good for us. Geordie seemed to read my thoughts.

"We'll go in and have a look at it. If the roof's not in already," he said, "we may have time to build our packs."

"Not all the packers have stayed at home, though," he added as if trying to alleviate my fears, "so it can't be that bad."

Reluctantly, we picked up our jackets and piece bags and made our way to the production face where we were collected in the Main Gate by the Deputy at the bottom of the run. Looking about, taking stock, we could see that the face-line rose some hundred and fifty yards to the top end, at a grade of approximately one in six.

"What's the situation?" Geordie asked the Deputy.

The Deputy was the regular for this face and should be well acquainted with the conditions.

"I've got to get the coal cutting machine on its cutting run up the face," he said, nodding to the machine which was lying in the road ahead. "There's a couple of packs to go in at just over half way up, that you and the young man can get on with whilst I'll keep Rab here to help out with the brushing."

He then walked off and left us. A man with lots of problems, I was thinking, and if it was left to me he could keep them.

"The quicker we get started the quicker we'll get finished," said Geordie.

Jackets were taken off again, and following behind him I started crawling up the face-line. It was laid with jigger pans, which were still at the moment; the roof overhead was sandstone and looked pretty solid with packs for support in the waste. The run was supported mainly with wooden props and straps, and the floor looked clean. If you can call a face-line clean, that is. Getting to where the packs had to be built it was immediately obvious that finding any materials to build them was going to be difficult, there was little or nothing we could put our hands on. Looking at the previous packs we could see that a wooden pillar had been built at both ends and the middle in filled with rubble.Geordie remarked that it would be a doddle if we could get our hands on some pillar wood and when the Deputy came on the scene, Geordie collared him. "As far as I can see there is nothing here to build one pack far less two."

The Deputy nodded in agreement.

"I know, I know," he said a bit impatiently, "now, you go ahead and do what you can, I'll see about the pillar wood."

Then he was off again. He doesn't hang about much.

After the Deputy left, we agreed to work together and build one pack at a time, using old wood and coal from the face. The Deputy wouldn't tell us to use coal for the packs, it's not done, it could be the cause of spontaneous combustion, but what else is there? Perhaps that is why he didn't hang about, he didn't want to be seen giving permission. Geordie crawled over the pans onto the face-line and with a pick started to take down the loose coal. I stayed in the waste to make a start to the pack. Shortly after, whilst shovelling coal over to me, he stopped.

"Listen." he said, looking in the direction of the Main Gate. "Can you hear that?"

Before I could answer he said, "It's the machine, they've started to cut."

He was still for a moment, thinking.

"We'll carry on for the time being and when the machine gets close to us, we'll go for our piece and let them get on with it.'

Geordie was attacking the face again and I climbed over the pans to clear his feet. By this time the machine was getting closer and I noticed that the coal was bursting off the face on its own.

When I pointed this out to Geordie he said that it was only the coal taking the weight of the roof. I wasn't at all sure. If the coal was taking the weight of the roof it must be on the move, and that I didn't like when I was below it. By this time, it will have dawned on the reader that I am not that experienced with dicey sandstone roofs. It is to be noted that when I left the pits to join the Air Force I was only an on-cost worker with little experience in filling and drawing, and when I came back I worked mainly on development and stone mines. I thought I should tell you that in case you might think that I was a bit squeamish. Anyway we stopped and went for our piece, and left the machine men to get on with it. Sitting in the Main Gate we were joined by Rab who wanted to know how we were getting on with our packs.

"Not so good," Geordie told him. "The face is clean, nothing to build with, but we'll get pillar wood and, with the machine cutting up, there should be plenty cuttings, enough to do."

Rab volunteered to come up and give us a hand out providing he was finished in time. We finished our pieces and made our way back up the face. The coal had been cut but the cuttings, lying six inches deep on the floor, made it difficult to crawl forward without slipping back.

I noticed that there was a difference about the place. The wooden supports were solid and pushed deep into the wooden straps. The coal was spitting out at us and falling from the face.

Geordie crawled on ahead seemingly quite unaware of the changes. Me, I'm on high alert ready to take off if necessary.

We had just reached our packs and sat down for a breather and we could hear the machine churning away at the top end. Then it happened. The machine stopped, all was quiet, listening, listening, then a crack like a gun being fired, a roar, a clatter coming from the top end. The whole face seemed to shake. I've never been in an earthquake but that's what it was like to me. The two machine men appeared from the top end coming at a fast rate.

"Run," they were shouting, "Run."

I needed no second warning, nor any encouragement from Geordie. I took off down the face in a flash, jumped into the pans, sliding face down, arms stretched out in front, going as fast as the pans would allow me. The noise was thunderous, cracking, as stone ground against stone, creaking as the wooden timbers took the weight. I didn't see any of this. My eyes were closed, I didn't want to see. I was aware that Geordie was behind, me close on my heels and the machine men not far behind.

I heard them calling. "Keep going, keep going." As if I needed any encouragement. I glanced up, saw lights ahead, four of them. Great, I thought. I was at the bottom end, the lights must be the Main

Gates. But they weren't. Four face-men were scrambling up towards us. With a great sense of relief I knew these were our guardian angels coming to rescue us.

I was wrong again. They came abreast and without stopping scurried on up the face-line. "You're going the wrong way," they shouted, "the face is closing behind us."

I was stunned, shocked. I grabbed the side of the pans and was sliding, my hands hurting, which brought me back from my daze. Leaping from the pans I caught my trousers on a ragged edge, which held me. I tore at my trousers and swore at the pans.

"Let go, you bastard."

It worked. I got free. I started up the face-line and noticed, to my despair, that I was being left behind. It seemed that it was every man for himself. I'm still in red alert, I hear nothing, see nothing, I take off up the face-line using my elbows, hands, knees and feet all working at the same time. The more I hurry the less progress I'm making. I'm slipping and sliding on the loose cuttings. My hands and elbows are taking a battering but I don't feel anything. Then I realised with relief that I was catching up with the men ahead.

They were bunched at the machine and had to crawl over it in single file on their stomachs. I caught up with them just as Wee Geordie was getting on to the machine. The man in front of him was holding us up, his lamp cable was caught on the control handle.

"Move it," I shouted at him, "Come on, move it."

I add a few other words which you've probably never heard before. Now, if there is a stage above 'Red Alert' I'm in it. If there isn't, then I've invented a new one.

Finally, we get over the machine and scramble up to the top road and relative safety. The Deputy was in the top road when we arrived, he'd been there all the time, while we were running the gauntlet. Wise man.

We flopped down on the floor to get our breath back, the four face-men having carried straight on out the top road, heading for the main gate. My breath was coming in gasps, and I was trying hard to control it, but I needn't have bothered. We were all in the same boat.

Sitting there in silence trying to get over the scare my mind went back a few years, whilst serving with the R.A.F, when I had a very similar experience. The roof banging away brought back memories of anti aircraft flak, shells exploding outside our aircraft, blinding red flashes and balls of black smoke.

The Deputy was talking, which brought my mind back. I'm wondering if the others are as scared as I am. They don't show it. The Deputy asked Geordie what the situation on the face-line was. That angered me. I couldn't believe what he was asking. What's the situation on the face-line? Does he really expect an answer? Does he think that while we are fleeing for our lives that we will stop, look around, and take stock?

I said, "Get your fat arse down there and look for yourself if you want to know."

I didn't really, but that's what I felt like saying.

The Deputy was talking to Geordie again.

"Just hang on a while until the roof settles then you can go down have a look at finishing your packs."

Am I hearing this? He wants us to go back down the face and finish our packs. The man's crazy. I watch Geordie and hear his reply.

"If you allow the machine to cut any more before we get our packs built, we'll not be going back."

I'm thinking Geordie has flipped his lid. I'm gutted, I can't even raise an objection. The machine men are looking on in some amusement. Me, I'm tickled to death - they are all fucking crazy.

After a while the roof did settle down. Meanwhile the Deputy had been down to the main gate and told us that nobody was hurt, and that Geordie and I should join him on an inspection of the face-line via the top end. I follow on behind them as they went down the face. We got as far as the machine and looked down, squinting through the haze that was hanging about. It looked like a disaster, a bomb site. The roof had broken off at the face and was sloping steeply towards the waste. In parts it had come down on the pans flattening them. The whole area looked like a Christmas scene covered by white powdered sandstone.

"That's it, a salvage job," remarked the Deputy.

Geordie nodded in agreement. I'm delighted. We can go home now. Turning back up the face, the Deputy pointed out that the ventilation was sluggish. A road would have to be opened up to allow more air to circulate and prevent a gas build up, and the face-line must be closed further down. It would be some time before this face could be opened up again and I had the feeling that we would get the job. We did.

That face had not finished with us yet. A few weeks later, after we had got the face salvaged and back into production, we were called back again. Not another cave-in, I'm thinking. I've barely recovered from the last episode and I'm not at all keen to have another go at it. It was nightshift again, which means coal cutting and you know the rest. On our way to the section the Deputy was explaining to us that it wasn't as bad this time. They always say that. They try to make things a bit better than they are.

"Its just one bit down, and it's falling onto the pans," he said. "A couple of shots should clear it off."

Walking into the section I noticed that the packers were all sitting in the main gate and they had no intention of going into the face. They were all smiling.

"The cavalry has arrived," one of them shouted.

If I had a gun I would have shot him. I was wondering why we should go on to the face if the packers wouldn't. You know, I have said it before, we didn't have to go onto the faces. It's dangerous and daft, but we did, and why? I'll never know the answer to that.

Whilst we were peering up the face-line into the darkness, the Deputy was explaining what had happened and what he wanted us to do. Apparently, the roof had come down, was standing virtually upright on to the pans. We would require to get the borer, which was at hand, and drag it up the face line with the drills.

Deciding to have a look-see before we did anything, which was normal practice, we began to crawl up the face and that was when I decided that stone miners must be rated at ten-a-penny and expendable, whereas packers were too valuable to risk on this type of work. Crawling up tight to the coal face we were soon to notice that so many supports had been set that there was little space to pass between them. We had to squeeze through, not a very nice situation should you have to get out in a hurry. The waste was closed tight. No wonder the packers were smiling, their job was done for them.

A little further on we came to the reason why we were called in. A bit of the post roof, about twelve feet in length had broken off over the coal line and slid onto the pans. The post was very thick and was resting on the floor taking the pans with it. The pans having been knocked over were partly under the stone and could not be run.

It was obvious that the stone would have to be bored and fired and only God knows what the result would be. If it was blasted off the pans, would the rest of the roof come in? Or, if sufficient were blasted off to free the pans would it be stable enough for us to work beneath it, and renew the damaged pans? That was the dilemma that faced us. One good thing, the roof was quiet, there was no movement. It seemed to have settled, and we hoped it stayed that way when we started to bore.

We hauled the borer up the face-line, threading it between the props and pulling up slack cable. It was an electric borer meant for boring coal and we knew that when boring stone the drill would shake a bit, so we set a stile against the stone to give us some protection. The stile wouldn't hold it, we knew, but at least we would get a warning should the stone start to move. A starting mark was picked into the stone to give the drill a start. I was holding the drill loosely in my open hands while Wee Geordie gave a few quick bursts with the drill and got a start. I moved smartly from under the stone and got behind Geordie to push on the borer as it was bouncing a little and shaking.

All the time I was watching, my eyes never leaving the roof. We got away with it and managed three short holes near the base of the stone, and I was delighted. If that stone had fallen on us we would have been taken home and posted below the door like a letter.

The holes were only about a foot long and we charged them with half a spat of ajax. When all was ready, the face cleared and all three shots coupled together, we waited.

What we didn't want was to hear a rumble when the shots were fired, just a little sharp crack would do us fine. The Deputy shouted

'Fire' and turned the key in the battery. We got our sharp crack and listened. No rumble. The air vibrated for a second, then all was quiet.

After waiting for ten minutes, we crawled back up the face. There was still some smoke hanging around but not enough to prevent us from seeing the result and my face from lighting up. The shots had done their job and the pans were clear. The conveyor would be able to run and be repaired should it be necessary at the next move-over. Feeling a bit pleased with ourselves we set off back to our own job, but not before a last word for the packers who were still in the main gate.

I felt like saying, "If you get into any more trouble just send for us we'll come and help you out."

I was to learn later that the miners who worked in this section had nicknamed it the Ghost Section and it truly earned its name. It seemed that the face would rarely ever be at rest, weird noises frighteningly like thunder far off, sometimes a loud crack like the fire of a rifle being fired, would cause all work to stop, the men on the face rigid, silent, listening, listening, ready to run if the rumbling didn't stop.

Most pits had their Ghost Sections. I believe the name was first coined at a pit called Brighills where the conditions were really bad, where the post roof varied in thickness from as much as twenty feet down to three feet causing very unstable conditions. I don't know what you would do but, since then, I have stayed as far away as I can from a post roof.

# CHAPTER TWO

## GLENCRAIG

I don't think that I was cut out to be a miner. Come to think about it, who is? Who, in their right mind would wish to spend the whole of their working life in the dark regions beneath the earth, where the sun never shines, in a place which has never seen daylight and never will.

In winter, men go underground before the sun has risen and don't come to the surface until after it has set. In spring, when the sun rises bright and warm it's wonderful, after a long cold winter. It's a pity that the brightness of spring can't wriggle its friendly warmth and freshness into the underground workings.

I can't think of anyone who would opt for such a life, but they do. Over sixty thousand men worked in the industry at one time and when you consider how many have been killed and maimed in pit disasters, roof falls, been buried, and blown-up in gas explosions, you realise that there isn't an area in Britain that hasn't suffered a major catastrophe in the long history of mining. So I'll say again, who is cut out to be a miner?

I was brought up in a Scottish village called Glencraig. Scottish glens are renowned the world over for their remote and beautiful isolation, each a little country unit on its own, walled in and surrounded with mountains which the eye never gets tired of looking at. God must have spent many pleasant moments creating these glens.

In early history, clans were formed, each with a chief, each with a different tartan by which they were identified. They even had their own small army. Many novels and films show the romantic character of the Highland glens, and places like Glenfiddich, where the romance comes in bottles. At the end of each glen there is always a castle, a landmark, the home of the laird, the protector of the clan.

Glencraig, however, was nothing like that, not by any stretch of the imagination. Well, maybe just a little. It was a mining village with rows and rows of miners' houses all blackened from the smoke of the coal fires. There were no grass areas between the houses, just dirt with wooden poles sticking out of the ground for the women to hang their clothes lines on when it wasn't raining, which could be a rare occasion.

We did say that Glencraig was a little like our romantic glens. It had a landmark that could be seen for miles and it was illuminated at night. It was the pit bing, and it was on fire.

Glencraig, divided by a burn into a north and south side, had a main street which was the only road in and out of the village. Both ends had a chip shop, a butcher and a pub. The chemist, baker and barber were on the south, with the Miners Institute on the north. That was it apart from a couple of sweet shops known as sweetie huts in amongst the rows.

The Miners Institute was where the men spent their free time, which wasn't much. They worked an eight hour shift, leaving for the pit an hour before starting and not returning till an hour after finishing time. That's ten hours in all, which didn't leave much time for leisure activities.

Glencraig was surrounded by other mining communities; you just had to stand on the Clune Hill and look in all directions to be confronted by pit bings. The pits all had curious names, some named after women, the *Mary* in Lochore, the *Nellie* and *Jenny Gray* of Lochgelly, the *Lady Victoria* at Blairhall, and others, the *Lady Helen* and the *Rosie*.

The men weren't left out either, names like *Michael, Francis* and *Lord Bruce*. Many were named after place names as in *Glencraig, Benarty, Bowhill, Thornton, Valleyfield* and on and on.

*Valleyfield* springs to mind because on the 28th October 1939, a disaster occurred underground in which thirty five miners lost their lives and many were injured with burns and carbon monoxide poisoning. Another pit in which I worked lost sixty men, one by one. Little wonder that the pits were thought of as dangerous. They were.

Miners accepted this. They knew the risks, they respected the dangers but were skilled at the work they did and could cope. The pits are all gone now. There are none left in Fife where there used to be fifty. To the west of Glencraig was all open countryside with a marsh and a forest, or maybe it is better called a wood. To the north, across the burn, is the Clune Hill and at the other side of the hill what was known as the 'Square Pond'.

It is now a large loch, part of a leisure park called 'The Meadows' (they don't half change things when you take your eye off them) and it was in this area where we, as school kids, spent all our free time.

In the spring, we would search in the marsh for ducks and water hens, eggs which we'd boil in a tin can and feast on. In the summer we would explore the woods and swim in the square pond, and in autumn, pinch neeps from old Dunc's fields. In the evening we 'Ploughed our weary way home', fearful of our reception awaiting us, our clothes smelling of fires, our hands and faces black especially around the eyes, our stockings and shoes in a mess.

We would take a detour via the burn where we would clean our shoes and wash our socks and dry them by thumping them over a boulder.

Our efforts, although not being successful, did manage to double the length of them, which you weren't aware of until trying to put them back on your feet. All this was done in an attempt to fool your mother, as if that was possible.

On your arrival at home, and the command was, "Clothes off, get washed and eat your supper." Head down, you obeyed without a word, and then, what you were dreading, "What happened to your socks?" in a much higher tone. Washed, fed, then you were off to bed, grateful that your mum was in a good mood.

I can recall 1939, the year that World War II broke out, a war that was to have a profound effect on the lives of people and although Great Britain won the war, she lost her empire and her place in the world. While her enemies, whom she had defeated, prospered, she went into decline. That same year I became fourteen and left school.

I had done reasonably well at school. I hated English, especially composition, but was able to grasp the mechanics of algebra. Maths I could get along with but art was what I liked most. It had always been that way since my primary school days.    At the age of fourteen, most boys would wish to follow in their fathers' footsteps and I was no exception. My father was a coal miner. It wasn't surprising, then, what I wanted to be, considering that I lived in a village where the coal mine was the only industry and virtually employed all the men. The young men, on leaving school, would go there for work.

It was generally known that to make a miner you had to start young. My grandfather had been a coal miner, and my father and my two elder brothers now worked in the mines. It was only natural that I would also end up as a miner.

I had a younger brother and a younger sister, both still at school, and we lived in the miners' rows, in a pit house which consisted of a bedroom and a kitchen cum sitting room. An outside toilet completed our estate. All the cooking was done on a coal fire which was never allowed to go out. It had to be kept going to dry out the pit clothes.

My mother was up at four thirty in the morning to prepare the sandwiches and flasks. The sandwiches were made up of two slices of bread spread with margarine and cheese, and two with margarine and jam. The flasks would be filled with cold water or tea, which would be cold by the time it was drunk. She would see the men off to work and get back into bed only to be up again at half past seven to get the children off to school.

When the men returned from work after an eight hour shift with the pit dirt on their clothes and bodies, she would have a large tub of hot water set by the fire for them to wash. They only washed the top half of their bodies down to the waist and wore long johns on the bottom half. The water was not renewed; the first to wash would get the clean water.

At meal times the workers would sit at the table and. the children would stand and 'grow big' as my mother would put it. It was at these evening meals that I was introduced to the mining language. My father and brothers would discuss the work they had done that day. I listened with interest as they spoke of 'pan-shifting,' 'stripping' 'packing' 'brushing' and many others. I knew they weren't what I thought them to be, but it didn't matter as I would know in time.

To get work at the mine the young boys would go to the pit yard, each day, at nine o'clock, where they would approach the surface foreman as he left his office to do his rounds. I was there at ten minutes to nine, dressed in 'hand-me-down' long trousers, with boots polished and hair tidily combed. At nine o'clock the Foreman, a Mr. McKinnon came out of his office and all the young men would hurry forward asking him for work.

McKinnon was a small round man, red cheeked, dressed in dungarees, black jacket, shiny black boots and with a cloth cap on his head. He would remove the cap and scratch his head a little before shaking it. "Nothing today, lads," he'd say and walk away leaving the boys staring at his back.

There were four young men in the group at the pit yard, when I first joined them. I didn't rush forward with them as Mr McKinnon appeared, I held back. I felt that I was a newcomer and should not get a job until the rest had been hired. A bit disappointed, I had expected to get a job right away. After a week, the answer was the same. "Nothing today, lads." My mother told me to be patient,

"After all," she said, "it has only been a week since you left school. You must keep going every morning to see Mr. McKinnon. Let your face be known. You'll get a job, have no fear of that."

That same day mother sent me to the colliery to collect my father's wages, which I did, and as I was leaving the pit yard I saw Mr. McKinnon coming in my direction. Timidly, I approached him and asked, "Have you any jobs, Mr. McKinnon?"

McKinnon, as he walked by, stopped, turned and said, "If you are fourteen and left school, bring your birth certificate to the office. You can start work on the tables on Monday."

I couldn't believe it, I just stood there, open mouthed.

Then Mr. McKinnon said, "Go on then, get it done."

I ran all the way home.

Word gets around fast in a small village and the knowledge that a boy, who left school a week ago, had been given a start at the pit was not good news to everyone. One mother shuffled her son off to the

*Expendable*


pit to confront Mr McKinnon. She got no joy, but left with a promise that her son would get a job eventually.

On Monday morning I was up with my father and brothers at four thirty. I was being ragged by them until my father put a stop to it.

"It's not so long ago that both of you were in his boots, so go easy on him," he said.

My eldest brother told me that I was silly to get involved in the pits, and that he had no love for them, adding that very shortly he would leave and join the army. "There's a war on," he said, "I'd rather be a soldier than be a miner for the rest of my life."

My father, who had been wounded in the 1914 war, listened for a short time in silence. Then he said, "War may seem to you youngsters to be all glory and manly, but it's a lot more than that. Men get killed in war, a lot more than are killed in the pits."

As we made our way to the pit, I stayed beside my father with my brothers walking behind in silence. It was still dark and it would be a couple of hours before dawn. Only the lights of the village showed some sign of life. A light breeze blew across our faces causing us to shudder. My brothers pulled their collars up around their necks. It wasn't the cold that made them cover-up, it was tiredness. They were hardly awake.

My father was talking; he was giving me advice on how to take care of myself and to do as I was told by the gaffer and to behave. We arrived at the check office. My father pointed to me.

"This is my youngem, it's his first day."

"Fine," said the checker. "Leave him with us. One of the table boys will take him up to Big Harry."

My father left with the parting words, "Take care, mind what I've told you."

Big Harry didn't get called that for nothing. He was a big man in his early sixties, who had been injured underground and hurt his back. Now he stood straight, as he couldn't bend easily. He could have been a Sergeant Major and in a way that was what he was to the table boys. He stood for no nonsense, was strict, but fair in his judgement and had a great sense of humour. I was taken to Big

Harry by a boy called Billy, who was a little bigger and a little older than I was. He had more beef on his bones, which he said was muscle. His patter and jokes kept us all laughing; always active and full of energy. We were to become good friends.

"What's your name, son?" Big Harry asked. I told him

"I know your father well," he replied, "and I have had your two brothers through my hands." He looked me up and down and smiled. "If you're no worse than they were you'll do."

He paused for a moment in thought, then said, "First we have to get you equipped."

He turned to Billy. "Take him down to the stores and have him fitted with boots and gloves."

As we started out for the stores Big Harry called after us. "Be back here pronto, the coal will be running shortly."

The tables stood some three feet off the floor, thirty feet in length, four feet across. The surface was made up of metal plates, six inches wide and four feet across spanning the width of the tables. It was a conveyor that squeaked, ground, and screeched with such a noise that, accompanied by the rhythmic thump of the shaker, which delivered coal on to the tables, it was virtually impossible to be heard.

The young men stood at either side of the conveyor removing the stones from the mix, allowing the coal to drop into a wagon which lay below the conveyor. The stones that had been removed from the tables were piled up on the floor behind the boys to be removed after the coal stopped running. It would be shovelled on to the conveyor and was very tiring for a new boy on the job.

Although I was keen and full of enthusiasm I felt very tired after each day's work. It was backbreaking bending over the tables, and especially tiring when shovelling the stones. That was where Billy helped; he took the brunt of the work. Big Harry, ever watchful, assured me that I would be fit and hardy in a few weeks.

I was barely coping with the work when I had my first mishap, while attempting to lift a large stone from the tables. I caught my finger against the side of the conveyor. I dropped the stone and tore off my glove. My finger wasn't burst but it was very painful. The nail on the middle finger was rapidly turning black and I could only work with one hand. When Big Harry noticed, he called me over and, after looking at my finger, advised me to go to the First Aid Room.

Near to tears, I approached the first aid attendant, Mr. Wilson, a man known to the miners as Mr. Fixit, as he had many duties and giving first aid treatment was only one of them. He was elderly, very efficient, impatient, and rarely smiled, and this was not one of those rare days. He examined my nail and sighed heavily. By this time the nail was black, thumping painfully with every beat of my heart. Mr. Wilson took me over to the sink and told me to turn my head away and not to look. As I did so my knees gave way under me; I almost passed out. Wilson had taken a pair of scissors and pushed the pointed end up inside my nail. I stood there shaking unable to speak or cry out as the black blood dripped from my finger into the sink.

"Sit down a minute, son," Mr. Wilson said, "I've done it the hard way so you'll get quicker relief."

He put a loose finger bandage on and sent me back to work.Back at the tables, I tried to hide my face from the rest of the boys as my eyes were wet. Big Harry, watching, called me over and said, "Sit down beside me for a while until you feel a bit better. You'll be alright tomorrow."

With the pressure let out I felt a bit better but my hand was still a bit sore. Big Harry said that if I came to work the next day, he'd fix me up with another job for a few days until my hand got better. The job I got was to be the graith boy; that was to get the miners' picks off to the blacksmith and get them sharpened.

As the weeks went by I grew much stronger, I could cope with the work and it wasn't so back breaking. I even began to enjoy it. The noise was still as great as ever and there was no improvement in the dust either. During this period, Billy and I became great friends. He lived a few doors away in the same village and we palled about together. When we got home from work and the weather was fine we, and a few other boys, would kick a ball around until we dropped. Laughing, tripping, kicking and falling over, it was great fun. Weekends, especially Saturdays, were our best time, with money in our pockets we couldn't wait to spend. It was two pence to play billiards in the miners' welfare where we spent the forenoon. Then in the evening, a wash up, clean shirt on and off to the pictures, which cost three pence.

After the show, a walk home to finish the evening with a fish supper in a bag and a bottle of lemonade; that was how Saturday was spent. Too old to be kids, and too young to chase girls. Sunday, just a day for walking, with no money left after the Saturday spree, so it was an early night and off to bed to get up at four thirty.

Picking the tables, as it was called, was generally a continuous effort to leave only coal and kept both hands busy. Occasionally, a load of stone would be dumped on to the tables, obviously a mistake, and when this happened it had to be shovelled off which wasn't much fun, and very tiring. Some days the coal flowed all day from the beginning to the end of the end of the shift.

During these heavy periods the boys had to take their break in relays, and only twenty minutes were allowed. There were other times when no coal was coming through, usually caused by a wreck in the shaft, allowing the boys to straighten their backs and stretch.

It was also a time for Big Harry to keep a close watch over his brood (idle hands, and all that). Apart for one or two, the boys were reasonably behaved. Big Harry's problem was to prevent the boys from leaving the tables and wandering unsupervised about the pit yard. Some of the older boys would fill paper bags with coal dust which lay inches deep on every surface.

They kept the bags out of Big Harry's sight until the end of their shift and then, from the gangway above the tables, they would let fly, striking the roof. The bags burst into a cloud of dust, showering every one who was left. They did not wait to see the result but made a dash for the pit yard and home; obviously great fun but not for those, including Big Harry who were left behind, coughing and spluttering.

However, they did it once too often. When the bags next flew Big Harry was ready, for as the boys reached the pit entrance, still laughing, there was a figure standing in their path; it was Harry. Having suspected what they would do, Harry had hurried to the pit entrance and got there before them. He got hold of the two ring leaders and took them aside, letting the rest go.

"Look both of you. I've a mind to recommend that you be sacked. You're teaching the younger boys bad habits; it's got to stop. Do you hear what I am saying? Do you?"

They only nodded with heads down.

"Right, now let this be a final warning. Next time it happens there will be a sacking."

They stood, head down, silent. "We'll leave it there, then." said Harry. He didn't get any more trouble from those two. Within a week they were both sent underground. What they didn't know was that Harry had a word with Mr. McKinnon who in turn spoke with the under manager.

"They'll sober up when I get them underground," promised the under manager, "otherwise I'll get rid of them. I don't have the time to baby sit Harry's youngsters."

The following Monday, before the coal started running, Harry called me over and told me to go to the blacksmith shop as I was now the new graith boy.

"Go on." Billy encouraged. "This is your chance to get away from the dust."

"What about you?" I enquired. "You've been here longer than me. Don't you want the job?"

"No," said Billy shaking his head. "It's not for me; I'm for underground It's about my turn and I don't want to miss it. Besides, there is more money in it."

"Okay," I said. "See you tonight."

He nodded. Picking up my jacket I made off to the blacksmith shop feeling very pleased with myself. I left behind some resentment from the other boys and one in particular, a boy called Francis, who was a bit of a 'Jessie' and a bully. He couldn't see why I, the last to start, should get the job. Harry explained to them that they would be going underground shortly and that I would be on the surface for some time yet.

Billy got his wish and went to work underground. We still met up at the weekends and had the usual fun. I was still only fifteen and being the graith boy was a happy time for me. My duties, apart from getting the men's picks sharpened, included being general message boy which gave me scope to travel all around the pit yard, getting to know everyone.

I also had to kindle the Manager's fire and have his office nice and warm for his arrival. I worked a lot in the blacksmith shop, where old Bob the blacksmith had been all his working life. An old man, he was fat, strong, white haired with a bald patch showing at the crown, and with a huge gray moustache. I liked him; he was a kind man who always would give me a 'pan-drop', which he was never without.

He kept the sweets in his pocket under his hide apron. He never spoke much and I couldn't tell if he was smiling because of his moustache. He taught me how to sharpen picks and how to temper the tips. I also was his hammer man. I found it a little difficult to handle the large hammer. I broke many of Bob's cutter shafts, but he didn't say anything; just got another shaft, and then would nod his head for me to try again. Most of the time my job with Bob was to keep the bellows going and the fire hot. I thought that Bob was a very old man and would be retiring shortly and I wondered if, had I been older, I might have taken over from Bob as the pit blacksmith.

I mentioned this to my father at supper one night, and my brothers laughed. "What, a fifteen year old blacksmith." they jeered.

My father advised me that it takes many years to learn all about metal and heat. "It's a job of love," he said, "That is why the old man is still working. He loves his job."

It was shortly after that, I got my second black nail. I had dropped a pick box onto my hand and I felt that this one was a bad one. One thing was sure, there was no way I was going Mr. Fixit. I suffered the pain until I got home. The beat, beat, beat, was the worst. When I got home father told me that I would have to let the blood out. He said that he wouldn't do it for me; that it was best done by myself.

He advised that a razor blade could be used to cut a 'V' into the nail until it bled. I started with a blade but found it too painful to cut into the nail. My father then brought a small drill and told me to what I did to get relief. I promised myself that I would be doubly careful in future.

Thinking back to something which happened at the pit, I realise I didn't know it then but was to think about it often in later life. The word futility was to haunt me for a number of years.

The weekend was always the best time for the table boys. It was a Friday and the boys were in a good mood. It was also pay day and that meant pocket money to spend. The morning shift had some two hours to go, but the endless squeaking, scraping and the roar of the shaker did not seem to bother us. We picked the stones from the tables, each with his own thoughts. Big Harry, as vigilant as ever, peering through the dust, casting his eyes over the whole room, was satisfied that everyone was doing what he should be doing, that all was well.

A pit head worker came down the stairs to the tables and spoke to Big Harry and then went off. Moments later, Big Harry closed down the tables and shut off the shaker. There was silence. Then, sober faced, he stood up on the tables, so that every one could see him.

"Lads," he said. "I want you all to put on your jackets and come over here and sit down quietly." One of the older boys asked what was wrong.

"I want you to be at rest for half an hour; then I will tell you what is wrong." Harry continued. "Now be at rest; no wandering about and getting into trouble."

We did as we were told, whispering amongst ourselves. We were to learn later that a man had been killed underground by a collapse of the roof. We were being kept at our workplace until the body had been brought up the pit to await the Doctor. There was uneasy excitement amongst the boys as we were sent home, hurrying to tell our parents but our parents already knew; the whole village knew. The men on the afternoon shift knew that the pit would be closed down for twenty four hours. That was the custom when a man was killed at the pit.

The neighbours would rally to the house of the widow to comfort her. Others would take the children of the family away to their homes so that they would not witness their mother's distress. Mining families in time of need knitted together to help where it was needed, but come Monday morning they would all be back at work as though nothing had happened, although, they will remember for a long time. I was told that a death in the mine was to be expected and miners accepted that.

When the boys were ready to be employed underground they had to be prepared for what lay ahead. This was done by attending the pit in the evening to be lectured on safety. Safety Classes were given by the under manager who, contrary to what was said about him, appeared to be a nice understanding man.

The lectures would start with statistics: the number of men employed: the tasks that they performed: the production of coal: the amount of coal mined to make the mine viable, and so on. The under manager would tell us that out of the one thousand men employed, only forty would actually produce the coal. These were strippers or coal getters, as they were known. He then went on to tell us of the dangers in working at the coal face especially to the young men known as wood boys who would supply the face workers with timber supports.

Throughout the lectures, which lasted six weeks, he would go over each operation underground and deal with the dangers involved. I was surprised to learn that of the thousand men employed a tenth were spare. This we were told was necessary to cope with absenteeism: injury, sickness and many other reasons. These men weren't really spare. They were employed on non priority jobs and could be called on when needed.

What stayed in our minds for a while was what he told us. "When you first go underground and step off the cage, stay in the pit bottom for a few minutes to get your 'pit eyes' and get accustomed to the dark."

# CHAPTER THREE
# THE MINER'S LIFE

We have already asked the question, what type of man wants to become a miner and spend the rest of his working life underground? No one that I know of, and yet there are hundreds of thousands of men, born and brought up in mining communities, who opt for such a career.

That may seem a contradiction, but I still maintain that, given a choice, the miner would have preferred a different occupation. He did have a choice, work in the pit or go on the dole. Anyone unemployed, in the old days, when there were so many jobs available in the pits, would be regarded as a social outcast. Miners thought that everyone should work for a living, pay his way and support his family, and they had no time for a man who was on the dole.

Recruit any young school leaver into the mines and you had a miner for life. Men joining the pits later in life didn't last as long.This was confirmed during the time I worked in the Longannet Mine, the largest mining complex in Europe. We needed many miners, but they were not available locally, and they had to be recruited from elsewhere.

Dundee was the place chosen to recruit miners, because linoleum mills were closing down and unemployment was high. The result was two busloads of men arriving at the complex to be offered work in the mines. They were given a meal, shown around the surface then interviewed. Quite a number of them accepted work but before the month was out there were only two left.

In this chapter, we are not talking about unions or the politically minded, our aim is focussed on the ordinary miner, a man with a wife and family to provide for, a man who rarely lost work and was as reliable as the pit horn, did his work, drew his wages and kept his thoughts to himself.

He was hardy, might even have been tough, knew that things

could be much better, but still preferred not to strike as it would cost him his wages and that was the last thing he could afford to do without. He was not a blackleg. When the pit was called out on strike he followed. He realised the union's point of view and knew that unions were necessary, as if through them only would wages and conditions get better.

He most probably would have entered the pit as a boy leaving school, working underground with his dad and eventually finding his niche at the coal face as a brusher. He would be constant backshift or nightshift and work along with the same team of men for years. He'd have the same piece made up each day, two on jam and two on cheese, washed down with a can of water. Outwardly, he seemed at peace with his world, but there was a longing in his heart for something better. He didn't know what it was but knew that it was beyond him, so just carried on.

At home he was relaxed. On the backshift there was no early rise, no rush, and he was fed before he set off to work. His children, on the other hand, didn't see much of him, because when they were up for school he was still in bed, and when they came home from school, he was at work. When he got home at night the children were in bed. He worked a five day week and did manage to see his children at the weekends.

He would spend some of his free time in the Miners' Institute where there were ample activities for miners to get involved in. The institute housed a card room where miners played a came called co-can, (I think that's how it is spelt) a game similar to Rummy where two packs are used and six men can play, each with thirteen cards. There was a reading room, a billiard room and a function hall. No alcohol was allowed in or on the premises.

On a Sunday morning the miners would gather where the tossing school was held, behind the bing to avoid police raids which happened frequently. It was a matter of 'heads I win, tails you lose' which took care of any money left in your pocket after the Saturday night outing in the pub. That was where he would have a few pints of beer to clear his throat, but he would rarely if ever get drunk, except on special occasions. When it was time to go home he would buy a half bottle of Four Crown wine to take home to his wife, at a cost of five pence. Women were not allowed in pubs in those days. Every village had a football field where the local team played their matches. Glencraig had a good team and so had Lochore, and they were great rivals, fairly equal in points in the amateur league so when they played each other it was always a match to watch.

The football field was situated a few yards from the houses and there was no excuse for not being there. Our man would be there as it would be most likely that one of his workmates played in the team. Of course, the football park would also be used for other functions; the big day in the summer was the children's gala when the kids would parade through the village streets behind the pipe band, all dressed in their Sunday best with a tinny, an enamel or tin cup, hanging from their neck, secured by a piece of ribbon.

Arriving at the football ground, they would sit on the grass in long lines and were issued with a mince pie, a bag of buns, and a small bottle of milk or lemonade. When they took the empty bottle back they would be given a brand new penny.

To add to the day's excitement, the fun fair would be there, not exactly Disney World but a few stalls nevertheless. The pipe band would play all day marching up and down the field, and a grand day would be had by all, especially by those who were winners in the races. Our man would be there along with his wife, of course, to keep their eye on their children, and even although they had been there the whole day they, too, would enjoy themselves, watching the kids in their excitement. It was the only time in the year when they could spend a whole day with their children.

The weather had a huge influence on people's lives during their time off and away from the pit, at the weekends, as it was able to curtail their outdoor activities, especially on a Sunday, their one day off. Most would be out and about, fishing, kicking a ball about, gardening, although gardening was not the way a miner would choose to spend his Sunday. It was too much like hard work, of which he had plenty. On a rainy day it was his lot to sit at home and look out the window. There was no television or hi-fi then.

It was one of those days. I was looking out the window of my bedroom watching the rain pouring down. It had been that way all day and I got fed-up and looked about for something to do. It was then that I spotted my brother's air rifle which he kept in the cubbyhole along with the lead pellets. I put a pellet in the gun and looked around for something to aim at. It was not my intention to fire the gun; it just didn't feel right unless it was loaded.

Looking out the window I saw a large crow some twenty feet away sitting on the next door neighbour's chimney pot. I opened the window slightly, poked the rifle out, took aim and pulled the trigger. The gun did not fire, it wasn't cocked. The crow still sat there heating itself from the fire below. I cocked the gun this time, took aim and fired.

To my astonishment the crow croaked loudly and fell down inside the chimney. I stood there for a moment staring at the empty pot. I couldn't believe that I had fired the gun. Then, realising what I had done, I quickly pulled the gun in, closed the window and put the gun back, then sat on the bed and waited.

I hadn't long to wait. From outside there came the sound of a commotion. Looking out the window I was just in time to see the children from next door running from their house, coughing and spluttering, waving their hands in the air as though to ward off some attacker. Clouds of soot came billowing out, followed first by the crow, then the mother and father who, with a newspaper in his hand, was thrashing the air attempting to get the culprit. The crow, being released from its terrifying experience, gladly flew away over the roof tops, trailing a dark stream of soot behind it.

It was not until later, when I heard my mother and the neighbour talk of the incident, that I learned of the damage that the crow had done. Apparently, the family was at peace, sitting around the fire, mum knitting, dad with his newspaper, when the crow made its appearance, followed by a cloud of soot. The crow, being more frightened than hurt, flew around the room hitting the walls, ceiling and windows, leaving its mark on everything it touched.

"Oh yes," my mum agreed, "It would take a bit of cleaning up."

"I don't wish that to happen again." exclaimed the neighbour.

My mum wasn't to know that it was her son that was the cause of the fiasco, and I wasn't about to tell her. To this day, it has remained my terrible secret.

Miners were in employment from the very beginning of our history, when it was found that coal could burn. Even before the time when monks dug coal out of the hillside, coal was being used. After the monks, coal was then taken from bell pits. This was possible because coal outcropped to the surface and it was just a matter of digging a shallow hole in the surface to reach the outcrop. The coal was taken out by pick and shovel from around the bottom of the hole, as far as it was safe, and the hole became bell shaped.

These pits were normally on a farm land and provided fuel for the farmer and his workers. There were quite a number of them, because whenever it was unsafe to continue to work in them or they became flooded, a new hole was dug. The coal was brought out of the pits by means of a ladder, by young boys and women with baskets on their back. It was gruelling work and it lasted until long after deep pits had been sunk

It is to be remembered that it was coal that started the Industrial Revolution and made Britain great. And it was that same revolution that made the demand on coal which started off the employment revolution, where hundreds of thousands found jobs in the industry.

More men were employed in mines that in any other single industry in the country and although coal would put food on the miners' tables it did not lift them any higher on the social scale. In fact, in a way, they slipped down a few points. Mining was then, and still is, a hard and dangerous occupation, and can be a life sentence for a young man who joins his father in the mine and remains working underground for the remainder of his working life.

But what of the miner's wife? She, most probably, would come from a mining family and know only other miners' families. That slim young girl, the pride of her father's eye, would marry a miner and spend the rest of her days in a life of drudgery, every bit as hard and tiresome as her mining husband.

She had been taught to cope with the hard life ahead, even from the earliest time when she was old enough to dress herself. She would have to work about the home doing household chores, learning to cook and bake, looking after her younger brothers and sisters, being of great assistance to her mother, whose work load was forever and endless.

That young girl, for all her chores would still be far better off than her grandmother. In grandmother's time, it was virtually the dark ages for miners. She would marry and set up a home in someone's spare room with the adjoining door being closed off, furnished with only a bed, table and two chairs, a piece of linoleum covering most of the floor, which was either wooden floor boards or stone slabs, and any carpet she could lay her hands on would be made of rags, torn into strips and woven by hand into canvas. All meals had to be cooked on a small coal fire and food had to be bought by shopping each day, as fridges were unheard of.

Water for household chores and washing had to be brought into the room in buckets. She would have an aluminium bath tub in which to wash her clothes and to have an occasional bath. It would be used every day by her man, who came home black from the pit.

His pit clothes had to be washed regularly and you can well imagine the state of dirt they would be in. He would normally wear a dark vest, known as a 'peeweep,' a dark shirt and trousers, heavy socks and pit boots, boots that were made especially for miners. All these dark clothes helped to hide the pit grime. Of course she would not have the modern soap powders, whiteners or washing machines, it would all be done by her hands, on a washing board.

Her wash day was a hassle and it lasted the whole day from early morning until dark. She would constantly hope that through her day the weather would stay dry. The washing was done in the wash house, a separate building situated between the miners' rows with each wife having a different day.

My mother's day was a Thursday, when the dirty clothes would be taken to the wash house and put into the boiler. She would then fill it with water and light the boiler fire. That was done in between getting my father off to work and getting the children up for school. We hated wash day as my mother was never in a good mood while trying to cope with father's dinner, him in from the pit and us coming home from school, and all the while running back and forward tending to her wash. It was not our best day of the week.

When she was younger there would not be such things as flush toilets, only dry toilets, built some distance away from the houses. The mind boggles if she were caught short in the middle of the night, especially in the winter. A potty, maybe? The midden was where all the household rubbish was dumped. Can you imagine the stench in that area, and the refuse was not removed until the middens were full to overflowing.

There was little chance of a miner's wife getting her hands on a little extra money, and no bingo or even a lottery to bring in a winner. The only source available to her was to join a money club. A woman in the village would recruit twenty others to pay to her one shilling (five pence) a week for twenty-one weeks, the names were drawn out of a hat to establish a rota from one to twenty-one, with the first turn given to the organiser for her work.

It is not hard to work out that each woman in turn would receive twenty shillings, one pound, which was a fortune in those days. Nor is it difficult to work out that the woman who drew number twenty-one would be anxious that the women who had already been paid out would not default in paying until her turn came up.

The miner's wife was always short of money, her husband's wages being only just enough to provide the essentials of life, but she would cope. With a house of children to feed and clothe, it wasn't easy. Porridge was a great favourite, and it would keep too. I have heard stories of Granny making a pot of porridge, cooked until solid, wrapped in a towel and put away in a drawer until it was needed. It could then be sliced and served.

Tatties and mince was also a great favourite, and I suppose it still is. Even to-day I still like it. Then there was vegetable soup with a lump of beef for stock which was later taken out and cut up and served with potatoes and peas. Great. Another thing, we never ever toasted fresh bread, it had to be hard to be toasted, especially the outside of the loaf. I can remember shielding my face with one hand and in the other holding a toasting fork in front of the fire. We didn't have toasters then, but it was all worth it, toast never tasted better that when made in front of a fire.

I've already told you the type of house we lived in, a room and a kitchen; two beds in the kitchen, mum and dad in one, four kids in the other, two at the top and. two at the bottom. The other bed was in the room, and that was where the older ones slept. Never well off, barely enough money to buy food and pay the rent, not always having a penny for the gas meter, sitting in the dark, the only light to see us off to bed was from the fire.

You can't be blamed for thinking that I am laying it on a bit thick, I suppose I am, but it's true. No money for toys, except once a year and that was at Christmas. A toy would be of tin, pressed into the shape of a gun, or for the girls, a rag doll. We also got a hanky, an apple and an orange, and if we were lucky, some caramels put into our stockings. No meals out, well, maybe a carryout from the chip shop, but that was rare. As for holidays abroad, the nearest thing to that was a picnic to the meadows or to Loch Leven and you had to walk all the way.

Miners did get holidays even then, one week without pay. Think of it, what the hell were we supposed to do on a week's holiday without pay and no money? Eventually, we did get a holiday pay, one week off and given five pounds. Just five pounds, and I know families who give their kids more than that to go to school. Anyway it was a start and then, just as miners became much better off, there were no pits left.

I suppose that people were more religious in those days, the church being nearly full each Sunday. It was, I suppose, all they had to help them with their arduous work and fear of dangers, for God was the only one who they felt could help. When it came to putting money in the plate, the Catholic church had the rest all beaten. Each parishioner was given a small envelope, into which they would put their weekly contribution and hand it in to the church. The priest, from the pulpit would read out what each family had given. It went something like this. "Mrs Stewart, two shillings Mrs Brown, two and sixpence."

Mrs Brown would acknowledge this with a slight nod of her head.

"Mrs Hunter, five shillings."

That wiped the smile of Mrs Brown's face, and all the wives would turn their head to look at Mrs Hunter, sitting two rows from the front looking smug. The wives all knew where she got her money, with her man on constant nightshift so she could keep a lodger. The church was being forthright in announcing the amount they had collected and at the same time letting everybody know those who had not paid a penny without saying as much. Very crafty.

It all seems such a wearisome life for grandparents and parents, as it is remembered. There was no radio or television, no dashing off to Spain for them. No, it was stay at home and make the best of it. However, they did find time to have a little enjoyment even although it was only a cup of tea and a scone with the neighbours, the women folk, that is, and they would finish this joyful event by reading teacups. You know the sort of thing. 'You are going to receive a letter from abroad and it could be good news' or 'A stranger will come into your life, but beware if he is wearing a black hat.'

My mother read cups and I have heard she was good at it. I think the whole thing is silly yet people do make a living out of telling your future, can you believe it? But after saying that, well, it gave them something to look forward to. As Robert Burns put it:

> 'An' forward tho' I canna see,
> I guess an' fear.'

Later on, miners were very much better off economically and physically. They were healthier, better educated, with pit head baths and pit clothes supplied. They were able to push off to far off places, even as far as Australia or Disney Land in America. They owned their homes, and had a car in the garage so, yes, a great difference from their grandparents' time.

When deep shafts were first sunk, the owners, in order to recruit men to work in their mines, had to build houses, Miners' Rows as they were known, for the workers. It was a great incentive in those days, a house and a job, couldn't ask for better. But there were conditions attached to the tenancy. First you had to work in their mine, and then the house had to be kept clean and tidy.

Animals, such as hens and rabbits, could not be kept in the house, and the owners had the right to inspect the house to ensure that the conditions of occupancy were not flouted. It is to be believed that the owners had their reasons for such conditions, as many of the miners were recruited from the hills where hens and animals had the run of the house. It could still happen. Here is an example. When I married, a long time ago, more that fifty years, we lived in the miners' rows and one day when I came home from the pit my wife told me that she'd had a visit from a hen. She said that it came into the house and picked around for crumbs, and when she gave it a piece of bread it went away. I didn't know what to say to that, but I did know that one of our neighbours, a few door away, kept some hens, in the garden, of course.

My wife insisted that it was always the same hen that visited. What could I say, except maybe, the next time it called to stick it in the pot. I think the hen got word of what I had intended for it, as my wife then didn't see the hen for some time. I had never seen it, and maybe that was why I was a bit sceptical about the whole thing.

One Saturday morning, though, when I was sitting by the fire reading, I heard my wife calling to me, in a kind of whisper, that she had visitors. I looked to where she was pointing and my surprise was complete, for there, wobbling into our house, was a hen, closely followed by four little yellow chickens. It was a wonderful sight; the hen had brought her family to for a visit. As I looked at my wife, she nodded and had a smirk on her lips, as though to say 'Now do you believe me?'

Of course, there is nothing new about plant owners building houses for their workers. Robert Owen built houses for the mill workers in Lanarkshire and his first village store became cradle of the co-operative movement. Not being content with that, he started the first nursery school, for his workers' children and evening classes for his workers. We couldn't keep this man in Scotland - he went off to America and did the same thing over there.

But let's get back on track, I think we will agree that to be a miner's wife was not a great ambition to aspire to, indeed, with her work load she would have been much better to be a miner herself. Well, not a miner as such, but women did work on the surface on the picking tables, not so many years ago.

But then, all that was stopped and only office workers, cleaners and canteen workers were employed. With all her workload one wonders how the miner's wife managed to waken each morning to get her man off to work at four. The answer to that was, she paid two shillings a week to a chapper-up, who would knock on the door with his stick at the time you wanted to be wakened and would continue to chap until he received an answer, to confirm that you were awake.

There is much, much more to tell of the life of a miner's wife, than I have told you here. However, I can tell you that she was the master in her own home; she ran the house, paid the rent, did the shopping, washed the clothes and ironed them, cooked the meals, fed the children, and a hundred other tasks.

Come to think of it, things haven't changed much. Women still are the bosses.

I will finish this chapter with a bit of nostalgia and I have no doubt that the old folks, like myself, will confirm what I am saying. Could you believe that when I was a young man I could buy a suit of clothes, a dress jacket and trousers, for thirty shillings (£1.50) and at that price, we could afford to buy a new suit every year. A pint of beer cost sixpence (3p) cigarettes cost two pence for five (1½ p) and for the sum of three pence, you could take home a fish supper in a pock. If those prices were still the same today we would all be millionaires. The school children of today get more pocket money that a miner got then for a whole week's work underground. It's a different world now.

# CHAPTER FOUR
## PAN ENGINE BOY

It is always a frightening experience going underground for the first time. Your young mind never ever associates the shaft with underground, nor do you realise that you will be three hundred and ten fathoms below the ground, below the pit head, below the village the fields and the burn. The realisation suddenly strikes as you step onto the cage and the gates come down to shut you in.

The cage starts to descend into the darkness of the shaft. It's wet; the water drops from the sides onto the top of the cage and finds a way inside. You hunch your shoulders to keep the cold water from your neck. The knuckles of your hands are white as you grasp the handrail. There is a silence in the cage although the cage is full of men. The only sound comes from the rush of air and from the cage as it rumbles on and on down the shaft.

There is a sudden 'oosh' as the other cage passes on its way to the surface. You stand there rigid, holding the bar, hoping the bottom doesn't fall out the cage. Your thoughts are running away with you. It can't fall out, can it? Before you can think of an answer to that, the cage starts to slow then jerks, the rope stretches, your stomach is in your mouth, your knees feel funny, you swallow, but never let go your hold on the bar. The cage starts dropping again then comes to a sudden halt. It has reached the bottom.

The Pit Bottom is lit, but not as you imagined it. It is small with the floor, sides and roof all come together to form a square tube like structure which stretches into the darkness beyond.

While I was talking about the shaft I remembered an incident which I think is worthwhile telling. It highlights that a disaster can be caused by a simple mistake, a moment of forgetfulness, a mind on other thoughts.

At the end of the shift when the miners are being brought up the pit and the cage arrives at the pit head, the banksman, as he is known, pushes a lever which causes two stops, or shuts, to protrude into the shaft under the cage, this device prevents the cage from dropping back down the shaft before the men get off, and the next shift of men get on. On one occasion, when the shuts were in position and the cage full of men ready to go underground, the banksman signalled to the winder to drop the cage, forgetting to remove the shuts. You can well imagine what happened next, the winding rope became slack, coiling down on top of the cage and bunching into the yard.

The bnksman realised his mistake, and started hauling on the lever in an attempt to remove the shuts. The men in the cage seeing what was happening were shouting at him, "No, no, don't," but he kept pulling.

There was panic on board the cage, the men at the front trying to lift the gates, struggling, pulling, hauling, yelling and they eventually managed to get out. Throwing the banksman hastily aside, they stopped the winder. Out of the cage the men scrambled, shaken and white, murder in their eyes but too much in shock to do anything. They all, to a man, went home and nobody stopped them. If the struts had been removed, the cage would have dropped like a stone to the bottom of the shaft.

Arriving at the pit bottom and stepping from the cage, who was standing there? None other than the nice under manager, the same man who gave the safety lectures.

"What the hell are you hanging about for, get into the section and get to work."

Not a great welcome for my first day underground. After being bawled out, which raised a laugh from the men, I was taken into the section by a young man whose job I was to take over. He was the 'Pan Engine Boy' and he seemed pleased to be relieved. He was a big lad, strong, well built, a bit of a weight lifter and he chattered all the way to the Deputy's station.

He carried a huge lamp in one hand, and an oil can in the other. His snack was in a bag slung over his shoulder. He took large strides and I could barely keep up with him, I was glad when we reached the Deputy's station, which was more than a half mile away. I felt warm and clammy and a bit out of breath.

*Expendable*

The Deputy greeted me. "Your first day son; not to worry, we'll look after you. I'll come and see that you are alright." He turned to the big fellow, whose name was Sam. "You'll stay with him for the whole of the shift to get him used to the conditions, and show him what to do."

We were then passed into the section. We walked and walked seemingly never coming to an end. Sam talked and talked, telling me all the things that I would have to do tomorrow. I didn't feel very happy about the big lamp or the oil can and I was very warm.

Arriving at the coal face it looked dark and frightening and it was very low in height, just over three feet. Sam crawled on to the face calling on me to follow. As I did I hit the roof with my head and fell back. Sam just laughed.

"Get on your knees," he shouted "and keep down."

The face line was about two hundred yards long. To the right was the coal seam, and on the left, a set of pans which ran the full length of the face-line. The 'pan-run' as it was known was made up of metal chutes ten feet long and bolted together, and jigged back and forward by the arm of the pan engine, which was situated half way up the face-line.

Left again were the stone pillars which were built like a dry-stone dyke and in-filled with smaller rubble. Built twelve feet long, twenty yards apart, they went all the way up the face-line. The packs were a support which allowed the roof to cave-in between them, taking the pressure off the coal face and providing infill for the packs.

We crawled up the face-line with Sam in the lead. The coal had been undercut to a depth of four feet and the cuttings, lying six inches deep in the track, made it difficult to get a footing. Sam had a piece of rope round his neck and on it he hung his lamp. He also carried his oil can in one hand, leaving the other free to crawl. I was doing my best to keep up with Sam using my knees, elbows, hands and feet. My hard hat kept falling off and my snack bag was catching on the roof.

I felt utterly out of place. Whatever had I let myself in for? We were alone on the face as we were first to arrive. It was very dark and we could only see what our lamps showed us. There was utter silence except for a strange creaking noise coming from the coal face and an occasional burst as the roof settled onto the coal.

We reached the pan-engine which was on the waste side of the pans and, crawling over, sat down. It was only then that I realised how frightening the whole place looked. All around, half the timber supports were broken. As I sat there listening to the creaking noise coming from the supports under stress I was thinking that the whole roof was about to cave-in. Sensing how I was feeling, Sam began talking to me, which brought me away from my thoughts.

"When the engine starts up you won't hear anything, and the roof will not collapse today - it will come down behind us as we advance, tomorrow."

Lights could be seen coming up the face-line; they were on the helmets of the strippers who would go to their usual stint which was ten yards long and four feet deep by three and a half feet high. They would strip to the waist and have a can of water close by. As I was observing all of the goings on, Sam had been explaining to me what I was supposed to do. I listened.

"You have nothing to do, only sit here, and when given the signal turn the handle and the engine will start up, when you receive a second signal turn the handle again and the engine will stop, simple. Okay?"

I nodded. Sam settled down, pulled a book from his snack bag and showed it to me.

"Tomorrow you would be wise to bring a book with you. You'll be here for eight hours, and with the heat and the constant noise you'll probably fall asleep. Listen, I'll tell you what I do."

I was listening. I couldn't avoid it, because he spoke in a loud voice.

"I tie a rope to the signal wire and the other end round my wrist and then, if I fall asleep, it wakes me when the signal is pulled."

The signal was a pull-wire from the loader end and when pulled it lifted a hammer at the pan engine to fall on to a waggon buffer. The hammer rose and fell once; the engine was started and began to jig the pans back and forward on their roller bases. It was very noisy.

Sam, seemingly not aware of the noise, settled down to read his book while I sat motionless with eyes and ears wide open. This was to be the longest day of my life.

The deputy came alongside as a shot was fired. I almost jumped out of my skin, tensed up as I was like a sprinter on the starting blocks. I was unable to relax. He assured me that everything was normal. Only three hours into the shift, and he had come to take Sam away, saying that he needed Sam to do another job, but that he would be back soon.

However, Sam never came back. The deputy did a few times, smiled to me and gave me a wave. Left to my fears and dreads I wondered why I had ever opted to go underground and leave the job I had on the surface.

When Sam had left he had given me his book, with the parting words, "Read it, it's all about sex."

Reading a book was the furthest option on my mind. I just stared at the hammer, willing it to chap and when it did I willed it to chap again. When it was stopped the silence was eerie, more frightening than the noise of the pans. I just sat there on the floor with legs outstretched, my back resting on an upright timber support.

"Will this day ever end?" I wondered, "Can I make some excuse to get back to the surface? I can't tell them than I was scared; what will my father think, and my brothers? No - I will have to stick it out."

After a while I saw lights coming down the face. As they passed the men waved and hurried on. Then there was no more lights to be seen, looking up and down, nothing. The pans were still jigging away with no coal on them. Could this be the end of the shift? I hoped so. The deputy came down the face-line, stopped for a moment, gave a wave then carried on down. Sam had told me that the man at the loader would chap five and that would signal the end of the shift. I had no idea of the time. I felt that I had been there for days and still I sat staring at the hammer. I jumped as the hammer raised and fell five times.

That was all I wanted. Stopping the pans I picked up my lamp and bag and made my way down the coal face as fast as I could. I saw no one; everybody had gone. Hurrying out the Main gate to the deputy's station I breathed a sigh of relief. The deputy was there waiting for me.

"Let's go home," was all he said. I couldn't reply. I had a lump in my throat.

Later, that would never have happened. Boys were not allowed underground until they were sixteen and only then after they had been on a six weeks training course at an Underground Training Centre. A boy certainly would not be put on to the coal face on his first day underground. Only when he was older and had received training for face work on all five operations, for a period of six months and more, would he be allowed to work on the face. He would probably be twenty one or older by then.

I had been the pan-engine boy for some months and had got used to the dust, the noise, the broken supports and the shots going off. I also had read the sex book three times. I knew each of the wood boys; they would call to me on their frequent runs up and down the face-line with their loads of timber for the strippers. I would watch the strippers, hewing out the coal, at ten yards per man, approximately ten tons per head, which had been marked out by the deputy.

As they took out about a yard of coal they would support the roof with a 4x4x2 inch wooden strap and two uprights, like a set of goal posts. With their head protected the rest of their stint of coal could be taken out putting up a set of goal posts every four feet.

If the roof was not good, they'd set a single upright to a short piece of strap until they had enough coal out to put up a set of goal posts. There was many a friendly argument between the strippers and the wood boys as to the amount of supports the stripper could have. A chew of tobacco was the usual price for an extra strap and a tree. The wood boys were restricted to the amount of wood they could take up the face-line, due to the height available.

The head boy would decide the amount of wood each stripper would get in order to save as much as he could to give to the men at the top end of the run. That way, the men at the top end would be wooded-up first, leaving the boy less distance to travel on their remaining runs. The method the boys used to transport the timber up the face-line was simple and effective. They would spread themselves out twelve feet apart and toss the timber from one to another. Thus the timber would travel about forty feet a throw. Even a greater distance was achieved when working in a stripper's stint. He was unable to work at the same time, so, he would give them a hand in order to get rid of them fast. A huge amount of timber was needed to keep the face going each day, so they would work with a day in hand which was essential.

At the end of the dayshift there would be a new track on the face-line where the coal had been hewed out. On the after-noon shift, the pan shifter would dismantle the pans and transfer them into the new track and advance the pan-engine. The packers, also on the afternoon shift, would support the roof with their packs and withdraw the remaining timbers from the waste to allow the roof to collapse.

Finally the nightshift, the brushers or strippers, would enlarge the roadway by boring and blowing down the amount of stone that the face had advanced on dayshift. The rubble would be packed at either side of the roadway and a circle arch girder erected for support. This was done at both ends of the face-line, namely the top road or tail gate and the Main road or Main gate.

At this time the machine men, the coal cutters, would undercut the coal to a depth of four feet. The coal cutting machine was a very heavy unit and required a strong chain to haul it up the face-line while cutting. The face would then be ready for the strippers, taking a whole day for one complete cycle. Saturday and Sunday were set aside for maintenance and repairs.

Should some incident occur, such as a wreck in the shaft, a haulage accident, a runaway or even the loss of power, the strippers would not be able clear out their stint. The coal left in the track stopped the pan-shifters, the brushers, the packers and the machine men from getting on with their work, so the whole operation would be thrown back, and a coal production shift lost.

Many a time the oversman would throw his hands up in despair. Even though he was not to blame, he would still have the under manager on his back for the lost production. The under manager would have to face the manager who, in turn, had to find reasons to give to the production manager, and on it goes, all the way up to the top. That is where the buck stops.

When I was released from the pan-engine job, I gave the new boy exactly the same advice that Sam had given to me, because it worked, especially the book on sex, and told him about being jolted awake by the wire tied round my wrist. The next day I had to report to the deputy for my new job. I felt elated, in high spirits. Getting rid of the big heavy lamp, swapping it for a headlamp, was a great relief in itself.

I was sent to work with an old man called Mick, an Irishman. I was to be his wood boy. The first job consisted of carrying an eight-foot wooden bar and two six-foot upright supports

On the face of it I felt that I could manage. However, I had not taken into account the state of the roadway until I arrived, and then I wasn't so sure. It was at the tail gate of a working section, and the actual repair where Mick was working was a mile inby. At the beginning of the roadway a severe incline had to be negotiated, a grade of approximately one in three for a distance of seventy yards. The damage had been caused by a fault in the metals.

The roadway itself had initially been eight feet wide and seven feet high but, the coal having been extracted from both sides, it had given way to side and roof pressure, resulting in the roadway being squeezed to six feet wide and five feet high. There was no rail track in the roadway and all the materials had to be manhandled. Also, it rose slightly towards the face and dipped from right to left making it difficult to stand and walk. Although I was glad to get away from the pan engine, I didn't like the look of this place.

When we arrived at our work place, feeling a bit hot, Mick advised me to sit down, remove my jacket, and cool off. While we were seated, Mick told me what I had to do.

"Go out to the end of the roadway and bring up the bar. That will take you a couple of hours and bring you up to snack time; then you can go back for the two uprights which will be a bit easier on you, but first we'll have a snack."

Mick, for an Irishman, was not much of a talker, but he did tell me that the coal face was about a hundred yards ahead of us and looking in the direction he was pointing I could see that the road ahead was crushed badly.

"Will we ever catch up to the face?" I asked

Mick shook his head.

"No, they advance four feet and we advance four feet, and never the twain shall meet. But it doesn't matter. The section will close shortly and we won't have to catch up."

Mick rose to his feet and handed a rope to me.

"We better get started."

"What's the rope for?" I asked.

"The bar is a wee bit heavy; you'll need the rope to pull it up the incline."

As I started to go out the roadway, Mick called after me.

"Don't hurry and hurt yourself."

I found the bar at the bottom of the roadway. It was heavy. Lifting one end, I dragged it to the bottom of the incline. It was then that I realised why I was given the rope. I would need both hands free to climb. I tied the rope round my waist the other end around the bar and started to climb. After about thirty feet it dawned on me that this was not the thing to do. There was not much foot hold and I kept slipping. The front of the bar was gripping the floor.

I didn't like this. There must be an easier way. I was travelling only about twenty feet at a time, before having to stop to get my breath back, and when I did stop I had to hold on to the bar lest it slide back to the bottom. Eventually I got to the top by having the rope over my shoulder, thus lifting the front of the bar off the floor. Exhausted, I lay down. I could have cried, but, this being my first day, I had to make a good impression and, with still some way to go, I was determined to prove myself.

When I arrived at the work place Mick was working away.

"Sit down and have your snack," he said, "I've finished mine." He swung his pick he called over his shoulder. "Just relax, get your breath back, you'll get the hang of it in time."

I didn't need to be told twice to sit down. I ate half my sandwiches, normally there was never enough, and drank all my water. Sitting there, I almost fell asleep. It was Mick calling back to me that brought me to my feet and I set off to fetch the two uprights. I was pleased with myself that I had managed to supply a day's timber and glad when the shift ended.

Back home, after washing and eating dinner, I fell sound asleep at the table. My mother let me sleep for an hour before she woke me, but I could have slept for a week. I thought then that I knew why my brother had wanted out of the pits. I wanted out of the pits. I hoped that, when I was older, I could go into uniform like my big brother and my father. After a week or so, I was in better shape and coping with my work, which I still didn't like but help was at hand - the section only lasted another month. It had struck a fault, not unexpectedly, and closed down.

"It's St Patrick's Day," said Mick one day, "Come now with me and help me celebrate, we'll just drop into the Minto for a pint or two."

Normally, at the end of the shift, he and I would go home our separate ways. I didn't drink, so I tried to make an excuse but he insisted. I thought that maybe I could handle a half pint or two, so off we went still in our pit clothes, to the Minto bar. The bar man gave us a hard look, then served up Mick's order which was a pint of Guinness and a half pint; then, as an after thought, two whiskeys - Irish, of course. Me, I hate Guinness, and I could do without the whiskey, but, what the hell, it's St. Pat's day.So, there we were, sitting at a table in the bar, Mick doing all the talking and me doing all the listening. He'd lapse into a real Irish brogue whilst telling me of the lovely old Irish bars.

"You can go into a bar in the morning, with the lads, and stay there all day until the wife comes to hurl you home in a wheel barrow."

I don't remember much about getting home but I remember my mother meeting me in the kitchen with folded arms, asking. "What's this?"

"St. Patrick's Day." I mumbled.

"According to the state you are in, St. Patrick has a lot to answer for." I didn't eat my dinner, just got washed and off to bed.

# CHAPTER FIVE

## WEE, SLEEKIT, COW'RIN TIM'ROUS BEASTIE

There was some company, to lessen the loneliness, when I worked with the wood boys, and that I enjoyed. I had the benefit of their company and also I fitted in well, Altogether, I was more content. At snack time the boys would sit together in the main gate while eating their sandwiches. The conversation, obviously, was about girls and the Saturday dance. They asked me if I had a regular girl and I lied and said that I had. When questioned further I just said, "The girl I fancy doesn't know it yet."

"We are all in the same boat when it comes to girls, we don't do the picking. They do." said one.

My eldest brother had joined the army. He was readily accepted which was surprising as mining was an exempt occupation. He had always hated working in the pits and couldn't wait to get out, and on the day before he left a family party was held for him. Well, not a party exactly, just some cakes and scones that mother had baked to feed the well-wishers.

We, my other brother and I, were proud that James was going to be a soldier. A few mates and his girlfriend were present all showing very different emotions: some envious, others feeling that he was mad, but all in a good atmosphere. Only Mum and Dad and James' girlfriend were more serious. My father, having been in the last war in 1914, hoped that his eldest son would not have to fight in the trenches and get himself wounded as had happened to him.

My mother busied herself serving tea and cake barely hiding her feelings. James was in a great mood, excited that he was, at long last, getting out of the pits, wearing a soldier's uniform and having a real gun to shoot. He was up early the following morning with all the good-byes done, and having spent the last evening with his girlfriend. Then he was off to the train station with my father. He never really got free of the mines, though, as he, along with other mining volunteers, was sent off to Gibraltar, and spent the war years tunnelling into the rock and building defences. James' leaving brought my other brother, Maurice, and I closer together. Previously I had not been allowed to go out with him and his mates; they had thought that I was too young. Now, on a Tuesday evening I was allowed to go out with them to the dance, and on a Friday night to the ball which finished at one a.m. as we didn't have to work on a Saturday.

On the way home after the dance we would stop in at the local bakery and buy some freshly baked bread rolls, and feast on them with our weekly butter ration. We weren't the least sleepy and needed to do something, but quietly, as Mum and Dad were in bed asleep.

At about that time we had mice in our house and, like us, they could not sleep at three a.m. either, so they came out to search in our kitchen for scraps of food. They had often been caught in the trap, which was a bit sad. We would catch them in a milk bottle and, of course, set them free again. It was then that we decided to have a competition to find which one of us could catch the most mice.

Of course the problem here was, how did we know that we were not catching the same mouse over and over again? Then I came up with a brilliant idea. As a bit of an artist, I had a box of water colours.

"We'll paint them," I said.

"Paint them?" Maurice asked. "How, and with what?" He looked puzzled.

"You know, with my water colours." I said. Anyway, we agreed and set out our milk bottles

As well as mice in the house, there were many underground, even at the coal face. Surprising in a way, as the coal face keeps advancing, so the mice must, also. They are found all over the pit and we are often asked how they get to be underground. The answer, of course, is that they come down with the timber supplies, or inside empty hutches.

They are friendly little creatures and whenever a miner sits down for his piece they come on the scene, expecting to get a few crumbs, and they do. Miners feel kindly towards these little creatures who share underground with them. While the miner, being more fortunate, returns to the daylight at the end of his shift, the little mites would be left to spend their entire life in darkness. They can survive on almost anything; bark from the wooden timbers or cloth from your jacket. Miners have to carry their pieces in tin boxes. Otherwise the mice would have it. Blind as they must be, they are far from helpless. They can find a miner's jacket in total darkness and get into his pocket. It's common for a miner to put his hand into his pocket and find a mouse there

.Mice at the coalface seem to come off worst because of roof closures. Many are caught-up in these roof falls, and. get injured. I have seen mice with only three legs, others with huge scars on their back and some with no tails. Rats are a different story. Nobody likes rats and they are killed if spotted. I don't know why this is, but they have got themselves a bad name. May be it's a fallout of the bubonic plague of the old days or their destructive ways. How do they manage to live down the pit? By killing and eating the mice.

Robert Burns must have felt fondness for these little creatures when he wrote the following -

I'm truly sorry man's dominion
Has broken Nature's social union,
An' justifies that ill opinion
which makes thee startle
At me, thy poor earth-born companion
an' fellow mortal.

and again,

Still thou art blest compar'd wi' me
The present only toucheth thee:
But oh! I backward cast my eye,
on prospects drear'
An forward tho' I canna see,
I guess an' fear.

Back to our competition, I had decided on red for my colour. It had always been my favourite. Maurice chose yellow, and we even made up a score card. Catching a mouse was one thing but to paint it was a different matter. Holding it upside down by the tail, over the sink, we discovered the best way was to soak it rather than use a brush, as the mouse wriggled so much that our fingers were in danger of being bitten.

After a couple of weeks, with the competition well under way, our score was about even when it came to an abrupt end. One evening while sitting around the fire, my mother was telling Dad that the woman who lived next door was "not quite well." Her actual words were that the lady next door was "off her rocker."

She went on to explain that while she was waiting her turn at the butcher's cart, the woman next door was telling all the other wives in the queue that she had yellow coloured mice running around her house. When the others gave her a funny look, she had said that she was telling the truth and that she had some red ones also. My father said that she must be on the bottle, as there is no such an animal; red and yellow mice indeed. They both had a good laugh.

"Poor soul," they said.

Maurice and I looked at each other, Maurice nodded to me and we left the room.

"No more," he said.

A few mornings later, my mother caught a mouse in the trap she had set and it was yellow.

There were two dances each week, one on Tuesday and the other on Saturday. The cost to enter was sixpence, nobody over the age of twenty-one was allowed in the dancehall and there was never any trouble. The girls sat at one side of the hall and the boys at the other. They were all local and probably knew each other. No doubt, the boys for their part would have a girl on their mind, and would dance with her more often. If he was chosen by a girl, in "Ladies' Choice", he would invariably ask to walk her home.

The older boys prepared themselves for the dance, especially on a Saturday night, by dropping into the local for a pint of beer. Thus fortified, they would boldly invite a girl to dance. However, most of the girls didn't like to dance with a man who drank beer; the mere smell of beer on a man's breath just put them off.

I would go along with Maurice and his mates to the dance. They were both eighteen and would go into the pub for a pint on the way to the dance. They would leave me outside.

"You are too young to go into a pub," Maurice said, "and anyway, Dad will kill me if I let you in."

I didn't mind; I don't drink and I couldn't dance either, so none of it mattered to me, I just liked to be with the older boys - it made me feel that I was grown up.

I'd pay my sixpence to get into the dance and just sit in the hall and watch. Maurice didn't have a regular girl so we would walk home together. The Tuesday dance finished earlier and there would be no time to walk the girls home; it was off to bed to be up at 4.30 for dayshift. I continued to go to dances with my brother and just sit and watch. I was beginning to think that dancing was not that difficult except, some of the boys could turn their feet in an amazing arrangement of skips, shuffles and side steps. They could even do it while reversing. The girls seemed to understand and anticipate every movement the boys made. They all seemed so agile and fit, especially when dancing a quick-step.

The band always followed the quick-step with a slow fox-trot. I felt that maybe I could manage a few steps but asking a girl to dance was not so easy. Then it happened, a girl, whom I didn't know, but had seen at the dance before, and admired, her, walked across the hall, came up to me and asked me to dance. I was on my feet and holding her before I realised what I was doing.

" I can't dance," I said

She smiled. "Come on we'll try it," and off we went round the dance floor at a walking pace. I had never been this close to a girl before, it was exciting, and although we were dancing at a slow pace I was breathless. She was a beautiful girl, I thought, dressed in a short grey blouse decorated with red flowers and a grey skirt with red pleats. When the dance finished, I thanked her and walked back across the hall to where my brother and his mate were standing.

"Wow" Maurice exclaimed. "Who is the lucky boy then? Are you aware that it was Ladies Choice you have just had? That means that you will have to give her the return dance, and it's the last dance."

The band started up again and my brother advised, "Go on then, give the girl the return dance."

I was still not clear in the head as I walked up to the girl and, in a very serious voice said, "Can I have this dance with you please?"

She rose and was in my arms again. She pulled me closer.

"I can follow you a lot easier this way."

While we were dancing I didn't ask to walk her home, I only asked her if she would be at the dance next week. She nodded. "Yes, I always come here on a Tuesday."

On the way home Maurice asked if I had offered to walk her home.

"No," I replied. "She might have said no."

"Coward," Maurice was saying and he continued to talk, but I didn't hear him, I could think of nothing except the girl. I could still see her. Her perfume still filled the air, and I wondered if I was in love with someone when I didn't even know her name. I would see her again on Tuesday.

It was back to work on the Monday morning. I didn't mind this time, as I enjoyed working with the wood boys. There was little time to relax, we were kept at it. The timber, stacked in the Main Gate, at both sides of the roadway, had to be handled on to the face and stacked. The amount of timber to be taken up the face-line on a run was limited by the height of the roof and should not stacked in any place which would prevent the stripper from working but, in fact we deliberately placed the timber in their way so that they would give us a hand out and see us on our way.

Most of the strippers were a good lot and would help out without our being blackmailed but there is always one in a bunch who is rotten, who wouldn't help us out and wouldn't stop working to let us pass. He would even demand extra supports and take them. He knew we didn't like him and he didn't like us either.

Many a time, the strippers would give us a slice of bread. Because like most young lads we were always starving, and even a drink of their water, but not Big Binnie, as we knew him. He was big and fat, he'd sweat a lot and smell, shout a lot and swear a lot. We wouldn't take a sandwich from him if he offered.

*Expendable*

Swearing underground was just normal for most men, and when things went wrong, the air was blue with some of the words, many I had never heard before, mainly directed at inert objects. The funny thing was that if any of us wood boys swore within earshot of a stripper, we would get ticked off. It seemed like no swearing until you are twenty one, which was very difficult for some of the boys.

In the end I enjoyed my time with the wood boys. Work in the pits for young men is a continual learning process, starting on the surface, advancing to underground and to servicing jobs, where you stayed for many years, with the end product a job at the coal face. Where is a man's ambition? What a prospect, what a way of life.?

My next job was to be a drawer at the loading point at the coal face. This consisted of bringing in an empty hutch to the bench, slewing it around on a metal plate and bringing it in line with the full track. When the hutch under the loading point was full, I would push the empty one to replace it, then push the full hutch along the track to be coupled onto a rake which was a number of hutches coupled together.

My position at the loading point was to stand between the empty hutch and the bench, which was raised to height of three feet behind me. I had to be ready to push through when the loader man signalled. With the hutch in front and the bench at my back, I had little more than two feet to stand in. I was in this position when the roof caved in.

It happened suddenly. No warning, no time to run. I found myself trapped between the hutch and the bench, and being pushed to the floor. I felt I was being crushed and could hardly breathe. I didn't feel any pain; I just lay there as I couldn't move. I could hear the pans still jigging. The loader man had run off. The next thing I remembered, there were voices all around, and I was being dragged out from under the debris.

Four men were lifting the debris away from me and two others were attempting to support the roof, to prevent further roof falls. I was half dragged, half carried up the face line, a bottle of water was pushed into my mouth, and a chew of tobacco to make me sick, and stop trembling. It worked. The Deputy arrived and dressed the cuts

*Expendable*


and bruises. I was examined for broken bones, and when none were found, they got me to my feet and made me walk out to the roadway. There was no stretcher in case I would think I was dying. On the way out, all my work mates were shouting words of encouragement, which gave me a lift to last as far as the first aid room on the surface.

Mr. Fixit washed and bandaged my wounds. This time he was more gentle, and kept assuring me that all was well and there was no need to call in a doctor. At home, my father told me to take a couple of days off until I felt a bit better. I was washed, given a clean gown to wear and sent off to bed, where I slept until the following morning.

The doctor called and gave the all clear. No bones were broken and he advised a couple of days rest. To this day I still carry the miner's blue scars on my back, shoulders, and thighs.

Because of my accident I didn't get to the dance on Tuesday, as I had hoped. I thought I would not see that girl again, I still didn't know her name and I had never told her mine. It would be a long time until next Tuesday. On the Sunday I went fishing with Maurice, but I wasn't paying much attention to my line. I was thinking of Tuesday. Maurice read my thoughts.

"You know, there is a parallel between fishing and women," he told me, "when you hook a fish you play it and bring it in to do what you like with, either keep it or throw it back. It's the same with women. When they know that you are hooked on them, they will play you on a long line until they decide to bring you in, and you don't know if they will keep you or not."

On Tuesday we were off to the dance, paid our sixpences and walked into the hall. The dance was in full swing and as I sat down my eyes were everywhere looking for the girl, for I believed that she would become my girl. Then I saw her. She was dancing with a curly haired young man. I saw that they were dancing very close and they were laughing.

She never looked my way and when the dance was finished the young man walked her across the hall to her seat with his arm around her waist. I thought they were arguing.

The band struck up again and whilst the other boys were quickly across the floor to get a girl to dance, I hesitated for a moment and when I made up my mind to go for that girl I was too late. She was already on the floor. I missed the next dance as well. She was dancing with the curly haired one again.

Eventually I managed to get a dance with her. The same closeness, the same perfume, I felt it was worth waiting for. I spoke little as I had to concentrate on my footwork, and holding her close was all I ever wanted to do.

She said, "I see you have made it tonight."

"Yes," I answered.

"I notice that you don't dance with other girls.,"

I was pleased as I realised that she must have noticed me sitting out.

"No, you are the only one that will put up with me," I replied.

She smiled and I was content just to dance with her. I was quite happy now that I had seen her again and danced with her. I was content to sit out the rest of the dancing and just watch. The evening was coming to an end when the second last dance, the Ladies Choice, was announced. I waited and watched. The band struck up a slow foxtrot; she got to her feet along with the other girls, to dance with the men of their choice. She didn't come for me, she chose the man with the curly hair. On the way home I was very quiet.

Maurice noticed and said, "Look there are plenty of pretty girls in the hall, you have only danced with one, once."

He kept talking but I wasn't listening. A few weeks later, my dancing was improving and I could manage most dances, nothing fancy, but I could get around the hall and danced with other girls. I made a point of giving that special girl a dance. She wasn't standoffish, she was friendly and nice and I hadn't given up on her. She knew how I felt about her and I sensed that she was teasing me a little. I was just happy to be near her. I now knew her name and she knew who I was. She still gave Ladies Choice to the curly haired boy, much to my disappointment.

But then, one Saturday night at the dance, I saw that she was not looking very happy. I also saw the curly haired boy. He was slumped

*Expendable*

on a chair in the corner of the hall, drunk. I gave her a dance and she asked if I would do her a favour.

"Yes, of course." I replied.

"I don't want to go home with him," she said, indicating the drunk in the corner.

"But of course," I replied again, holding down my excitement.

Before the end of the dance she signalled to me that she was about to leave and I saw the curly head was now sitting up and looking around. As I walked her home the drunk followed us for a short distance, then he turned and walked away. When we arrived at her gate she thanked me and I got a good night and a peck on the cheek, then she was off.

I stood for a little while, and thought that if she was my girl I wouldn't drink. I felt that now I might have a better chance with her, and so it happened. I got Ladies Choice regularly and we became great friends. I asked her for a date and she agreed. We went to the picture house, and for walks on Sundays, along with a group of other girls and boys. The curly haired boy never appeared on the scene again. She even took me to her home to meet her parents and family.

Her father was a miner, but in a different pit from me. He worked as a brusher, constant afternoon shift, and had been at that job for many years. I also met her sisters and brothers. The sisters made a fuss of me and I loved it and was happy in their company. She and I were very fond of each other and became sweethearts.

My brother James and my father were now both in uniform. James we would hear from regularly. My father, stationed with an artillery unit locally, was able to get home a lot. They were missed badly, especially when the air raid sirens were sounded, as Maurice and I, being Messengers, had to leave our mother alone at home with my young brother and sister.

At the end of our street a warden shelter was built where the local men, with helmets, arm bands and gas masks, would man the post, awaiting an air raid. The shelter was furnished with a stove, a table and chairs which the men themselves had put there. Should an air raid happen, they were to note the damage, make out a report and send it to headquarters, which was just up the road.

*Expendable*

The report was taken by a Messenger, a young lad who was recruited only if he owned a bike. He also had a helmet, arm band and a gas mask. There were never any air raids, and no messages to send. Eventually, the whole enterprise turned into a social meeting place for the older men. In those days people were very inventive due to shortages. They made lighters from anything that could hold a little petrol: a screw nut with two pennies welded to either side, or an aspirin bottle with the wick sticking out the top.

Everybody was doing something; women came into their own, with their savings and thrift. A blanket, dyed, made a fine overcoat, women started to bake bread again and scones, and there was a slogan, 'Dig For Victory'. Cigarettes were in short supply; you were able to buy five cigarettes but two of them had to be Pasha; these came from the Middle East, and were known locally as camel dung.

Fortunately, no bombs dropped within ten miles of our village. Nevertheless, a total blackout had to be observed and after being up most of the night, we were still expected to get up for work in the morning.

The war was in full swing. Maurice and I talked about it a lot and many a time spoke of joining up. I preferred the R.A.F. but Maurice was non-committal. He was not very sure of what he wanted to do. He was going steady with a local girl by this time and matrimony was more on his mind than the war. Then one day I went to the capital and volunteered to join the air crew with the R.A.F. I had a medical and was accepted, and a few weeks later I was called up. My girl friend was very upset when she knew what I had done. I couldn't give her, or myself, a satisfactory reason for joining up, I had just felt that I had to. I was seventeen years and six months old, and my mother said that I should not be doing this as I was only a child.

After the tears and goodbyes, my father took me to the railway station where I would catch a train to London. My father asked why I had decided on the R.A.F. I told him that while he was away I had joined the A.T.C. which in a way prepared me for joining up. During those dark days, virtually everybody was doing something for the war effort.

# CHAPTER SIX
## A NEAR THING

Leaving the R.A.F. after the war was over, I was flown home from North Africa. I felt a great swell of pleasure and emotion as I neared home, I had been away for more than five years and was looking forward to seeing my family, friends and most important, my girl. As I walked up our street in Glencraig, past the miners' rows, past the Miners' Welfare, I noted that the men who had said goodbye to me when I left were the same men standing there when I returned. The same blackened houses, the same chimney pots spewing smoke from coal fires, and the same grey sky welcomed me back home. Yes, already I was beginning to regret that I had left the R.A.F. especially recalling some of the lighter moments. I was thinking about one just then as I walked towards home.

All the 'Welcome Home Soldier' activities had been wound up. I was just another soldier coming home from the war. My father and brother were already at home and back at work in the pits. My brother, after spending five years in the tunnels in Gibraltar, was still determined to get other work. He eventually became an insurance clerk and later took over a public house. I had been given two weeks leave before returning to the mine, and I spent most of my time with my girl. We were planning to marry in the summer. Too soon, I had to report for work at a colliery.

I started work in the pit bottom pushing three empties which came off the cage to be joined on to a haulage and bringing back three full tubs, holding on to them for dear life, afraid I'd lose control of them and land up in the bottom of the shaft. The work was killing me. I was healthy, and tanned, but I wasn't fit, and cursed myself for going back to the pit. I was thinking of the good life I had known in Africa, where I was somebody, where the sun shone every day, and all the buildings were painted white, and here I was, back where I started, down a dark mine. I had almost forgotten what a pit looked like. I lasted only a week on that job and then other found work with my brother Maurice; he and I were always great pals. Work was about to start on a new surface mine, being driven from a field. This I enjoyed, getting underground wages for working on the surface. The weather was fine and we'd sit in a field for our snack. The job lasted six months, and then it was back underground, where I stayed with that same team of mine drivers for the next two years. Meanwhile, I got married and tried to settle down.

It wasn't easy. Restlessness filled the souls of those men who had come back from the H. M. Forces. I was fortunate. My wife was a very gentle and loving person, and she knew I was restless, even although I hadn't told her. She also had a great inner strength which would see us through the hard times ahead, wrestling with normal life after me being away for years in the forces.

I stayed with the team of stone miners for a number of years and we would travel to work in many of the pits in the immediate area, which were managed by the National Coal Board. I left them when my father, who had been contracted to drive a mine at a local colliery, asked my brother and me to join him. By this time I was a leading man and had my own team. When the mine was completed my father left and moved to another pit and most of the men went with him. I liked this pit and stayed on to develop the coal drivage.

My mate, Big Ken, stayed with me and with two other men, both local, and made our team up to four. We worked on three shifts with two other teams, also local men, and eventually drove and equipped a coal face. When all was ready for production, the strippers moved in and took off about thirty five feet in just over a week; that's about seven cuts. But, as usual, there were problems with new faces: problems with supplies, conveyors, transport and brushing, not to mention the shortage of manpower.

At this point, the roof didn't close, the brushing was three cuts behind the face, and there was little rubble for packs. The waste pillar wood was being used and because the brushing was behind, with no low side stow, it was taking two shifts to clear a shot of brushing and even then almost half the shot was being filled away.

It was decided by the powers that be that we would be called back into the face to open up the low side, to allow stowing. This was decided on the Friday and we were to start on Monday. As it turned out, the job that was ahead of us was to become a lot different to what we expected. On the Sunday afternoon, the Deputy, doing his inspection, went into the new section from the tail gate. Looking down the face, he could see that some fifteen feet down it appeared to be closed. On closer inspection he found that it was shut, and he couldn't go any further down the face-line.

Turning about, he made for the main gate, and when he arrived he was faced with the same situation. It was closed completely, from end to end. Everything, the pans, coal cutter and cable, was buried. The conveyor motor at the road-head was barely visible. Even worse, the air was sluggish, and fear of a build-up of gas meant that the section would have to be fenced off until ventilation could be restored.

Roof falls are commonplace in mines, which is easy to understand when some mines have as much as twenty six miles of under-ground roadways, which have to be inspected and maintained daily. It is little wonder then that the roof caves in. However, it is rarely that a coal face collapses from end to end. Falls occur on a face-line, that is true, but not with such disastrous results.

One face-line collapsed in a mine at Kirkcaldy while men were working. They managed to save themselves by sticking close to the coal face while the supports keeled over and the roof roared in, a terrifying experience. After the roof quietened down, two men who were thought to be lost, just walked out on top of the rubble, badly shaken but unhurt.

To return to our own face closure, the collapse was caused by a number of things. Of course, everybody knew the reasons, after the event, like closing the stable door after the horse has bolted. Everything had been in place for just such a happening. If they had wanted to close a face they had gone the right way to do it. The whole thing had been set in motion by the machine men, who had begun to undercut the face, starting at the main gate. At least that had been their intention, but about half way up the face line they had noticed movement and the face supports taking a heavy strain.

Stopping the machine, they had decided not to cut any more and called in the deputy. This information had been passed on and arrangements had been made to have loads of chock wood brought in on Monday to support the waste, but Monday turned out to be too late. Later when the ventilation was restored, we got the job of recovering the coal cutter.

We throve through the main gate, in advance of the face, a narrow road, coal high, for about twelve feet, then turned right parallel to the face leaving a pillar of coal between us and the face, and advanced to where the machine might be. This was worked out by the amount of machine cable still lying in the main gate. Then turning again we broke through onto the face-line. Surprisingly, we came out at the machine control handles. So they got something right.

At this time, I lived in a large village called Ballingry. There weren't any pits there and the mine I worked in was a fair distance away. To go by bus was an ordeal. There was no direct route. First you took a bus to Lochgelly then another to Kinglassie, so if you missed a bus you lost a shift. The best way was to cycle and that's what I did. Going to work is easy; you are fresh, fit and it's down hill most of the way. It's the coming home that gets you, especially after a double shift, and what happened one Monday.

We were driving a mine down an incline of about one in eight, to reach a coal seam. We had reached a point some fifty three yards from the top when we struck coal and so then took a sharp turn to the right in pursuit of the coal. A round of shots were fired, all the coal had to be hand filled into hutches, which were then, three at a time, being pulled up the incline by haulage. We were kept working with three further hutches, while the full ones were drawn up the incline.

Having a breather, we heard the roar of a runaway. The rope pulling the three full hutches to the top had snapped and they were on their way towards us at a fast rate. We had only seconds to move, and that's what we did, fast. We virtually flew across the road to the tight side and crouched down together in a heap. We hadn't even time to be frightened before the hutches were almost on top of us. They smashed into the pile of redd, striking and knocking out the face girder which just missed us, and then all was quiet. We got up

*Expendable*

as the haulage man came running down. He was very excited and could barely speak but managed to spout out, "My God, am I relieved that you are alright."

He's relieved. He's reading our thoughts. A broken haulage rope is a serious matter in the pits, particularly where men are involved, as in this case, and so it wasn't long before the deputy, oversman and under manager were on the scene, sympathising with us. The under manager offered us a double shift. This was a reward made to us to keep us quiet, obviously, but loyalty rewarded with hard work seemed a bit odd. As it turned out the hard work was in the canteen. Great, double shifts are hard to come by, and it's really the money that we are thinking about. But they never found us something to do and just told us to go home.

That incident was on Monday and on Friday, arriving at the pit, getting into my pit clothes I was surprised to see all the day-shift hanging about the surface making no attempt to go under-ground.

"What's up?" I asked the man nearest to me.

I was told that there was to be a pit meeting in a couple of minutes and that the delegate wanted to talk to us. I thought that he was going to refer to the Monday incident and we could be in trouble for not bringing the matter to light. The delegate, when he appeared, stood on a box or something to look over the heads of the men.

He was a tall man, elderly, wearing overalls and a jacket with a cloth cap on his head. I'd seen him before, and thought he was an official, but I was soon to learn just who he was. He had an office on the surface and spent his day between there and the canteen, never getting his hands dirty because he didn't have a job.

By this time my mates had joined me and we listened to the delegate telling us to go home to support the night shift who, for one reason or another, had come up the pit and then walked out. It was obvious that the local men knew why the night shift had gone home, but I live a thousand miles away and had heard nothing. The young men were delighted at a day off and were already on their way home. My team mates were of the opinion that if the men were going home then they must also go.

The meeting was over, the men returned to the baths to shower and change. I was not pleased, I had just arrived and now had to cycle all the way back home. Two things came out of this. One, I wouldn't lose any wages for today but was supposed to work a double shift on Monday and the thought of losing the extra money made me angry. Two, to make matters worse, the delegate didn't go home on strike. He finished his shift and didn't lose any wages at all. What kind of man would do that?

A new section was started up: it was a double unit with both ends feeding on to the main gate. The seam was only three feet high and the main gate was nine feet high, leaving a brushing of six feet which happened to be sandstone. It was a sore task for five men, what they had to complete in a brushing shift each night, and to make matters worse it wasn't to be supported by circle arch girders but by square work 9ft by 12ft, the reasoning being the main gate would eventually be a double track endless haulage.

Just imagine then how the brushers felt after a round of shots had been fired leaving a mountain of redd. The story goes that one night, after the smoke cleared, the brushers walked into the road head and, seeing the mountain of redd that had to be shifted, one of them said that he would have to go home as he had the cramps. From then on whenever the brushing was fired you got a chorus from the men, shouting, 'First for cramps!'

You are probably wondering why I should mention this brushing as we were not brushers, just simple stone mine drivers, but we got ourselves involved like this. The section had hardly started, just a few cuts taken off, when a small fault was struck, a step-up of three feet. Now this roadway had to be kept level; no way could it take a sudden jump-up, which meant a three feet high bench would have to be carried. This was turning out to be no ordinary brushing. Both top and bottom had to be fired, and the stow was three feet above level. Just as we were thinking that things couldn't get any worse, they did.

Because of the three feet jump-up the Main Gate conveyor could not be advanced to beneath the double unit delivery, which meant that a trench had to be blown to allow the gate conveyor to receive the coal. A headache? You bet. There wasn't enough time for the brushers to clear up and be ready for the coal production shift because boring with an electric borer was taking too long. Blast hammers were needed and that was when we were called in. We'd bore the holes for the brushers, clean up what was left, blow the trench and advance the conveyor.

All this meant that too many men were being used and too much time was being taken up. The powers-that-be wanted to know if fewer shots, heavily loaded with ajax, would bring down the brushing. A round of three shots was suggested to us but we didn't agree. We maintained that at least six shots were necessary, because of the width of the roadway, some twelve feet. We lost, and another team was brought in by the under manager to show us how. They bored three holes, fired them and left us to clean-up. It was a disaster: the brushing came down alright, in a solid block, nine feet by four feet by three feet, flattening the gate conveyor and knocking out two sets of girders. The structural damage was bad enough, not to mention the loss of production. In the end, we got our way and stayed with the brushing until, bit by bit, we lost the bench. It was then back to our own work.

You are probably wondering why I should write all this about a brushing road. Big deal, you might think. Well, there are three reasons. Firstly, I was a bit peeved at the under manager for failing to accept our method. After all, stone miners are a very experienced lot at blasting out stone, as many men are with the various jobs in the pit, strippers, brushers, packers, machine men, and a lot of others whose jobs are out with the face. It was no surprise to us when the under manager's idea failed; we even expected it. The second reason is that there is a moral to this story. That is, when a man is given a job to do, let him get on with it. Don't give him a job and then tell him how he should do it.

You may have noticed that I deliberately left out the name of the colliery where this happened. Don't think it was to protect those responsible, it was to protect *me*. Should the under manager know about this, he'll probably come and thump me. The third reason? I've forgotten.

The curious thing about this mine, which ran from the surface - no, that's not the curious thing, all mines run from the surface - was that at the bottom a large waiting area, or room, had been constructed. It was well lit and with bench seats round the walls, and was a place where men who had finish early could wait until lousing time , because no way would the man riding bogies be sent down early. This waiting area had a dirt floor which was smoothed and kept clean by the men.

So, with time on their hand awaiting lousing, the men played marbles, and they also played quoits using three inch washers. The waiting area was in two parts, one for marbles, the stone type, gorries, I think they were called, and the other was for quoits. It was quite something to watch these grown-up men playing schoolboys' games. They were good at it, and had partners, who always played together. To get a game you had to have a good partner and be pretty good yourself. It was a matter of getting your work finished and hurrying out to the waiting area to watch the champions at play. Now, isn't that curious?

# CHAPTER SEVEN

## JENNY GRAY

One day, I was standing at the top of Auchterderran Road in Lochgelly, waiting for a bus to go on backshift, when a man passed by on a bike, and as he did so, he had a look at me. It was Dempster Smith, manager of the Jenny Gray.

He stopped and called me over. You see, we knew each other, as I had worked in pits where he was manager. I told him where I was going and where I worked, and he offered me a job, saying that it would be a lot less travel for me. It was true, and I was getting a bit fed-up with these long days and with the daily travel. Even my bike had packed in, that's why I was waiting for the bus that fateful morning. I was flattered, and accepted. Anyway, I couldn't say no as I liked the man.

Now the Jenny Gray was unique. Never had I been in a pit that was so old fashioned. It must have been forgotten when coal pits were being upgraded. The surface layout could be described as normal with two shafts, of course, and the rest of the yard included a wood-yard, stores, engineering and electrical facilities and all those other bits and pieces which go to make up a pit surface.

There was one thing that I believe no other pit had, and that was a 'wheel brae' for wagons. Jenny Gray was on high ground with no railway out except the wheel brae. This was something to see; a twenty - ton wagon going down a steep incline for five hundred yards or more, while hauling up the empty wagon at the same time. One must wonder what would happen should a wagon run away.

Surprises didn't end there. Arriving at the colliery on my first day I asked a man, who turned out to be the under-manager, which shaft I should go down.

"Which shaft?" he repeated, giving me a funny look. "Any shaft, just get down the pit."

I started to tell him that it was my first day and that I had expected to be told where to go.

"Didn't you hear me? I just told you where to go," he said, without looking at me but over his shoulder. I was thus dismissed from his presence. Not a very good start for me on my first day, and things weren't about to get much better. I got to the pit head and on to the cage with the rest of the men. The cage moved a short distance then stopped and the men got off.

One man said to me "Are you coming?"

"No," I said "I'm going to the pit bottom."

"You're here!" he said, as if to burst out laughing. I knew it. This was not going to be my best day.

I stepped off the cage and heard the pit bottomer shouting. I turned around to see that he was talking with the banksman, actually shouting up the shaft. I heard the banksman reply. It was unreal; I don't know why they needed a cage, as they could have jumped down.

As I walked to the deputy's station, which happened to be in the pit bottom, I noticed a group of men arriving from another direction. They had come down the other shaft. Both shafts arriving in the same pit bottom led me to wonder how they arranged their ventilation. Yet more surprises were in store for me. The tubs, or hutches, were small; of an average length, but short in height which suggested to me low workings. The wheels were the strangest I had ever seen, just a round flat disc, like a washer.

The rails were angle irons, some four feet long and made of cast iron, which was prone to breaking. Instead of a flange on the wheel to prevent it from coming off the rails, as all rail transport systems have, the upright on the rails did the same job. It had to be seen to be believed. I was thinking that if that's the kind of equipment they worked with, what were the men like?

It was like moving back half a century. Many of the men were wearing 'yankee bonnets' which I had not seen for years and to see where they were going, carbide lamps. It certainly was odd; old fashioned, and I kind of liked it. I don't know, but maybe it was the red glow of the flame from the lamps, or it was the bringing back of old memories of earlier times in the pits. But I was at ease.

I was given a headlamp but was told by my newly acquired friend, the under manager, to get myself a carbide lamp, as headlamps were for officials only. Did you ever get the feeling, when someone was talking to you, that they were really talking to a piece of shit. That's the feeling he gave me.

Moving off, into the section, whilst being escorted by the deputy, who never spoke a word to me, I saw another strange sight. A flame, yes, a flame, coming from a tallow lamp. I'm not kidding, the flame was about two inches high. A flame is the one thing you never want to see in a pit, and yet here was one, on the head of an old man who was standing at the conveyor transfer point. I pointed this out to the deputy.

"It's old Davie," he said. "He uses a tallow lamp."

That was another first for me; I'd never seen a tallow lamp before. As we walked past old Davie, he nodded and removed his pipe from his mouth. He was smoking a pipe? Underground? Smoking? I was taken aback. This was one weird pit.

My day was not yet over. I was being shown around by the deputy, and I was to learn that this was being done on the orders of the manager, and that he, the manager, would deal with my work orders. Now I was beginning to understand why the under manager was acting in an aggressive manner, which was so unusual when, in general, under managers don't bother their shirt tail who starts in their pit. But I felt that he should get off my back, as it was not my problem.

Being shown up the face line, I was surprised to note, after what I was thinking, when I saw the small hutches, that the coal was almost six feet high, with wooden uprights and straps for supports. The waste was closing right up to the line of waste supports. The rubble seemed to be a mixture of blae and dirt, and I would shortly find out why. To my amazement, bees and butterflies were happily flying up and down the face-line.

You don't believe it, do you? I wouldn't either if I had been told, but it's true, and don't go thinking that this place is too much for me, and that I have flipped my lid. No, I'll tell you how the butterflies and bees are on the face-line: it's like this; the top road of the section was only six feet from the surface and in some places less. A hole had been punched through to a field in the surface and the men would sit in the sunshine to eat their piece. I bet you have never heard of that before!

There are other unusual things that happen when the workings are so close to the surface. You can hear a train rumbling by overhead, and when it rains you can be sure of a soaking underground the next day. The Jenny Gray sure was an unusual pit in more ways that one. The men were a bit unusual also. For instance, I was walking to the pit on a beautiful sunny day, and still a quarter of a mile away when I meet the backshift going the other way.

"What's up?" I asked.

"We are going home to lie in the sun," the young men answered.

"Strike?" I asked. "No, no strike, it's the best day we have had all year and we're not going to lose it."

Simple. There was no strike, it was just a nice day. I admired those young men for having the guts to do what they did. I can remember as a young man many, many times going down the shaft in Glencraig pit on a lovely summer day. It was heart breaking. But, then again, coming up the pit at the end of dayshift, and just as the cage neared the surface, where the sun was streaming down the shaft, to hear the shouts of joy, from the men in the cage, was something else.

So it was back home, to sit in the sun with my shirt off, thinking of the times in other countries where I sat in the sun. It was a day for a swim and a couple of pints, which reminded me of the last time I was desperate for beer. It was like this.

During the period when the RAF types were being transferred, from 15. S.A.A.F. squadron, to 500 squadron RAF, we were stationed at a place in Northern Italy called Villa Orba, next to a village, where the bars sold vino and vermouth only, which came in three colours, Red - medium dry, Rosa - a sweet, and Blanco - very dry. We drank mainly vermouth, half a litre at a time.

There were no dainty glasses of wine for us, and after a couple of half litres you knew that you had been drinking, especially when you started to wind your weary way home. There was no alternative to wine, no beer, not a single bottle, and how we yearned for a pint of draught beer.

We lived in tents and our camp was in a field where melons were planted. We helped ourselves to those, often. A hedge of vines bordered the field, so we were never short of fresh fruit, with all those melons and grapes and, of course, there came a time when the daily dose of fruit became too much. Between the fruit and the vermouth we all finished up with diarrhoea, upset stomachs and a 'drouth' that would drink a loch dry.

Fortunately, we were not doing any flying. We would not have been able. I suppose the excess drinking could be put down to relief of not having to fly bombing raids and be shot at in return. Anyway, whatever it was, it was good drinking and each day we would make a vow never to drink again. That was until the next night.

Flowing alongside our camp was an irrigation channel, six feet wide and between two and three feet deep. It flowed pretty fast and was reasonably clean. The local wives did their washing of clothes by the stream, and we used it by the bucketful to wash and shave. Even though the war had finished in Italy, we were expected to keep up a high standard of cleanliness and dress. The Commanding Officer demanded that we did. This stream was to become our main source of entertainment and fun.

One of our guys got hold of a small dinghy which he inflated, got into the stream and sailed away out of sight for about a mile, to where the channel split into two and was much shallower and stonier, but a mile was okay, long enough for fun. Within a very short time, everyone was in on the act. No paddles were necessary just find a dinghy and lie back and let the stream carry you straight down for a mile.

However, it got out of hand when two and four man dinghies began to appear and, once again, the Commanding Officer put a stop to our fun, mainly because the dinghies were being borrowed from our aircraft.

This was a period when we were being rested, over-rested according to some, and we were not allowed to know our next move.

*Expendable*

We wondered if we would be sent home or not, as the war was still on in France and Germany.

We didn't like the idea of moving to assist them, as we had fought and won our war in Italy, and thought that they should get on with it also, leaving us to carry on eating melons and grapes and drinking vermouth and being sick and suffering diarrhoea.

We got news one day that the Americans had captured a brewery a bit up north. Apparently these Yanks were keeping it to themselves because the brewery produced beer. This got us wondering and a meeting was held in the sergeant's mess to discuss how we could get our hands on a barrel of the stuff. It was decided that eight of us would travel up north in a three-ton truck, try and talk our way into the brewery, and then persuade the Yanks to let us have some beer. We took two special presents with us that had been donated by an officer, to help us bribe the Americans.

It took a few hours of travelling up north and another hour to find the brewery. The Yanks let us in without fuss, through the perimeter fence, which was guarded, and led us into a spacious lounge, advising us that we could drink all we could hold but that was it. There would be no takeaways. We pleaded with them that a whole camp of airmen was anxiously awaiting our return but no, the Yank in charge, a big burly sergeant, would not give way. We asked him what would he give for a bottle of scotch, the bribe we had brought with us.

"For two bottles of Scotch you can have the brewery," he beamed. "Get your truck backed up and I'll see what I can do."

As a result, a huge barrel of beer, the like of which we had never seen before, was rolled onto the truck. There was barely room for us to board but we managed with great difficulty and we put it down to the endless pints which had been served to us by a gorgeous Italian waitress. Come to think of it, she wasn't that beautiful before we started drinking. It's amazing what alcohol does to your eyes.

It was a long way back to base and the driver of our truck was doing his nut, as we hadn't allowed him to drink. Well, someone had to stay sober, but he did get one pint out of the barrel when we arrived back at camp. Halfway home some of us were getting a bit dry and had a need for some more beer. When we examined the barrel, we found that the bung was on the bottom and an arm's length away. We were just able to reach it and eventually loosen it, but how were we going to get a drink, with no mugs, and no glasses? We sat there looking at each other hoping for an idea to get at the beer. To pull the bung out would be a waste of valuable beer but we still wouldn't be able to get to it.

I suppose that in every group there is a clever guy or a head case, and we had one. He suggested that he would lie on his back head first and that we push him, by the feet, up into the space between the barrel and the side of the truck, next to the bung, and then move it slightly so that a trickle of beer would run out and into his mouth. We thought it was a crazy idea but if he could do it without losing any beer, it would be worth a try.

We got him into position. He could not use his arms as they were trapped by his side so one of us with a long reach had to remove the bung and bingo! It worked. When we pulled him out to let the next man in, he was soaked but with a smile on his face.

"Told you," he said, "I'll go to the back of the queue to wait my turn again."

By the time we reached camp, every body was soaked, including yours truly, but very happy. What a welcome we got. We were heroes. It was all hands on deck to set the barrel up in the field and then everybody sat up with their mugs full of beer, drinking well into the night. That is, all except us heroes, who had had enough, and were already sound asleep.

I was finding I was beginning to like the Jenny Gray, for all its quaintness. Maybe the word like is a bit strong, and I should just say that I was getting used to it. I'd wake up in the morning and go off to work without a care in the world. There are not many pits you can say that about, and the reason, I suppose, was that we were making good progress with the job we were doing, the management seemed to be happy with that and left us to it. Even the under manager didn't bother us, but then he didn't congratulate us either.

We were driving a mine twelve by eight feet, carrying a four foot seam of coal and a layered blae roof, when suddenly, after firing a

*Expendable*

round of shots, we came up against a solid wall of stone, with no coal. No one was sure where the coal had gone, up or down. We were told by the under manager, on one of his rare visits, that the coal would be upwards.

He said he had come to this decision by the angle of the fault. It was decided that we would back-up the road and drive a new drivage over the top of the old one, actually on top of the girders at one point. There was a lot of space below us and it could be used to our advantage by getting rid of the debris we were producing. We made a hole down through to the old drivage and dropped as much muck as we could. The making of the hole sounds as if we knocked a hole through from the top, but no, the hole was made from the old drivage, upwards, by means of explosives.

It was the manager's idea. I was given detonators and ajax and set them in the flange of two sets of girders. The shots did the job. The girders were broken leaving a nice gaping hole for storage and at the same time giving us something solid beneath our feet.

You would be right in thinking that firing the shots was illegal, as was breaking girders with explosives. But in those days stone miners were allowed a lot of leeway when it came to using and firing explosives. It was quite common for us to be given detonators to fire our own shots when a shot-firer was not available.

If you thought that was illegal, what about this: Many years later, when I was an official, the manager called me to his office. He seemed very agitated and angry.

"I want you to go down the pit right away and take the shot-firing battery from the under manager," he said.

He when on to explain that the deputy of the section had reported that he had found gas and had stopped shot-firing and cut off the power, but the under manager did not agree that the action of the deputy was necessary and had taken it upon himself to fire the shots. Meanwhile, the deputy had withdrawn the men from the face.

"Get down there in a hurry. The Man-rider is standing by, and take a methanometer with you. Give me a call when you get there."

I made my way to the section and was not happy. Just suppose the deputy was right and the place was full of gas. You can imagine what I was thinking. When I arrived in the main gate the deputy, the shot-firer and the other men were all there, expecting that at any minute, the under manager would blow himself up. When I told them what I had been ordered to do, they said that I had a big heart. But I didn't have a big heart, nor was I brave. I was shit scared. I have said it before, sometimes you do things that you never thought you would do.

There I was, crawling up the face-line behind the under manager, pleading with him to give me the battery. He shouted at me.

"Don't be bloody stupid! Read your methanometer and you will see that there is not enough gas to be of danger."

I *was* being stupid; in my panic I had forgotten all about my methanometer and hadn't even looked at it yet. So I looked, and the needle barely moved and then went back to zero. I tried again and the same thing happened. What the hell was I panicking for? And then, the next second I almost jumped out of my skin, as the under-manager fired a shot, which I hadn't expected. With my heart still in my mouth, I caught the battery he threw to me.

"There! You can take it to the manager now. I am finished with it."

Well, he said something like that but I can't repeat it as there may be children about. On the way down to the section, I started questioning why the manager was sending me on this suicide errand. Was I expendable? I knew a couple of others on the staff whom he could have sent and they would not have been missed. As it turned out, the manager, prior to sending me down, had spoken to the under manager, and all that I was doing was to keep the unions' faces straight. That was all very well but they might have let me in on the plot.

One particular deputy was finding more gas in the section than the rest of the deputies total findings. He must have been crawling about in the waste looking for it and so he was nicknamed 'The Gas Man' but not to his face because he was a *big* man. He was manoeuvred to night shift where he could do less damage to production, but still he reported gas, again and again. Three mornings on the trot he reported one per cent in the G.B. The manager had had enough, especially as the finding was made out on the pre-shift report, which was statutory and had to be kept for something like seven years. The manager decided to send someone down on night shift to check it out.

Who did he send? Come on, you know, it was me of course, with the final instruction to take a methanometer with me. On the night shift I met the deputy in the main gate. He knew I was coming. Nothing goes on in a pit without everybody knowing. The deputy was sincere about his findings and assured me that he was talking about gas in the G.B. and took me to the top road to the place where he took his measurements. He wasn't using his flame safety lamp, but a methanometer, which was not illegal, but it was less reliable than a flame lamp.

Anyway, what was a deputy doing down the pit with both a safety lamp and a methanometer? It was just not done. His machine was switched on and reading just over one per cent. I switched on my machine and the needle jumped, only to fall back to zero. I could see that he was about to argue with me, so I suggested he made a test with his flame lamp to see what he'd get.

"You can't see one per cent on a flame lamp," he said, a bit annoyed.

I was making a test for gas at the same time.

"See, nothing," I said. "I suggest that your methanometer is away out and needs to be calibrated, and I further suggest that you use only your flame lamp in future."

The methanometer was later sent to the laboratory where it was found to be faulty.

You are probably wondering just who the hell I was, that the deputies should listen to me. I've never told you this before but I was the wee man who trained them on gas testing and prepared them for their five year renewal exam. I suppose that was why the manager sent me down when there was a wee problem with gas and not, I hope, because he considered me to be expendable.

By the way, we did find coal again. It was up, about twelve feet up. I had a local man working with me, a young strong man, built like a horse, and a head taller than me, though that does not tell you much as you don't know how tall I am. He was called Chad Hannah, a very popular young man who was well liked throughout the pit. We were working in a narrow coal drivage, where there was only room for the two of us.

We'd fired a round of shots and filled it away on the conveyor, which loaded on to stationary pans. They lay on a slope of about fifty yards, and loaded on to the main belt below. Remember, we had found the coal up, so that then was the incline to the coal.

We had room for a set of supports but didn't have any to hand, so Chad went down to the main belt where the supports were lying and I continued to fill away the shot. On his way back up the incline, with the supports on his shoulder, Chad was struck on the head by a large piece of coal that flew off the pans. I found him lying, unconscious, some time later, at the bottom of the incline, when I went to see what was keeping him.

He was taken to the hospital and diagnosed with a fractured skull. That night, my wife and I went to the hospital to see him, stopping to buy a bunch of grapes on the way. Isn't it funny that everybody takes grapes to the sick in the hospital? I bet it was a fruit merchant who started that.

When we arrived at his bedside Chad was sitting up and smiling. He was already popular in the ward. When I gave him the grapes, he looked round.

"The next time you come to see me bring in a couple of slices of bread, they starve me in here."

Anyway, it wasn't long before Chad was back with me in our narrow drivage, and shortly after that it was my turn to get crowned, which was only fair, Chad having taken the first knock. We had just fired a round of shots in the coal, and when the smoke cleared, I took my pick and crawled into the face, Chad following close behind. Both of us were satisfied that everything was as it should be, with no supports blown out, the roof looking solid and a good four feet taken off the face.

Chad got the conveyor going whilst I started to dress down the face. Whilst pulling down the loose stuff, debris falling from the roof peppered my helmet. I immediately hunched my shoulders to protect my neck, but nothing happened. No more fell, and I looked up to see where it came from.

I shouldn't have looked up. The roof, as though it had been waiting for me to look up, came down. I was struck on the face, causing me to jump back, dazed, more by the suddenness than the hit. I was cut and bleeding from my nose and brow. Fortunately, it was near the end of the shift so we just packed up and made our way to the surface.

On route, we met the deputy, who gave me a dressing to hold on my face. He said that it was only a surface wound, but phoned ahead to alert the first aid room and also to the pit bottomer, to allow me quickly up the pit. Chad came with me and as we walked to the first aid room we ran into the manager. There we were, me with a blood stained bandage being held to my face, looking through one eye, no jacket and behind me, Chad, carrying my bag, helmet and jacket, and looking as if to say "It wasn't me, I didn't do it."

The manager looked a bit alarmed and asked what happened. I told him that I had been stupid, that I had been caught out.

"Get cleaned up and come and see me," he said.

Later, when I stood in front of him, I had plaster on my nose, eyebrow and brow, and also the first sign of a couple of black eyes. He offered me a job on the surface until I was fit again, adding a bit of advice, "Remember, people who don't do anything, don't get hurt."

I still have the blue marks on my face to this day. Our union man suggested that I should make a claim for the marks that were left and gave me an application form, which I completed. As a result, I was called to a medical board in Dunfermline public baths, to be examined by two doctors. One was a wee bit disappointed when I told him that I didn't wear glasses, which he had hoped would cover the scar on my nose. I was eventually awarded twenty six pounds.

As a miner you have got to accept that you are going to be hurt or injured. It happens all the time. I'm not talking about cuts and bruises, I mean hurt enough to be off work. Much later, when I was a Safety Officer at a colliery, I could record thirty accidents a month - that's one a day. It's a war down there, and you have got to look out

*Expendable*

for yourself and that only comes easier from experience. I have blue marks all over my body, most miners have, it's the miners' trade mark.

Of course you got compensation when you were hurt in the pit and unable to work but that didn't make up for the wages lost, far from it, but any pay was better than no pay. I recall a case where a man got hurt *outside* the pit and got paid compensation.

He had been at the miners' welfare on a Sunday night and after drinking heavily, he left rather late and on his way home fell and broke his leg. He was carried home and after being up all night, his mates carried him into the pit yard and then into the first aid room and claimed that he had fallen in the yard. I'm sure that the man, if he read this, would smile and confirm that it was true.

# CHAPTER EIGHT
## COAL AT A PRICE

Many years later, after 1963, I found myself at a colliery, which to spare its blushes, I will call Camdon. I knew little of that pit, but, I knew the manager, who I will call Mr. Smiley, who had been appointed to the job three weeks earlier. We had worked together in the past and I knew him to be a very efficient and dedicated administrator. Apparently, he had been sent there to do a clean-up job, as weak management in the past had allowed control to pass on to the unions. I didn't know the situation at that time, but I was soon to learn.

For the last twenty years I had worked in the training and safety branches of the Coal Board and had gained considerable experience in recruitment and wastage, and dealing with absenteeism. I was also the minute secretary of all the pit meetings. I was no whiz kid but obviously Smiley felt he could use me.

That first morning, when I arrived at Camdon Colliery, I parked my car in the car park and walked towards the pit yard. It had been raining and had now turned to drizzle. I stood there and took in the scene around me. The yard had a dirt floor and was uneven, allowing pools of water to form in the depressions.

It was a large square shaped yard with the whole of the south side being taken up with offices. To the east were the electrical and engineering workshops; to the north, two main shafts and behind them a very old slag heap. To the west lay the canteen, pit head baths, stores and compound.

The whole place looked as if it had been laid out at random, with the blacksmith shop planted right in the middle of the offices. The confines of the colliery were enclosed by a high wooden fence, with a large, central gate, also made of wood. It looked more like a stockade for a fort than a pit. It was barely daylight and in the gloom I thought it looked very depressing.

I was advised to wait in the canteen until the manager could see

*Expendable*

me, which I did, accompanied by a cup of coffee. The canteen floor looked like an extension of the pit yard. Eventually, the manager's runner came for me and we left the canteen, hurrying across to the yard, dodging pools of water to arrive at the 'Holy of Holies', the Manager's Office.

The morning meeting was being held when I entered and Smiley introduced me to those present. They were his two under managers, two chiefs, the storekeeper and the surface foreman. The morning meeting was to deal with the priorities of the day and never usually lasted very long. It was over within half an hour.

Smiley told the surface foreman to show me around the pit head but first I had to be given overalls and Wellington boots as it was still a bit damp out there.

"Come back when you're finished and we will talk," he said as I left on the tour.

The rain had eased off a bit by the time I returned to Smiley's office.

"Well, what do you think of our ranch then?" he asked.

I didn't think much of what I had seen but I didn't tell him so. I replied that it could do with some improvements, otherwise it wasn't bad.

He looked at me for a moment, then sitting back in his chair he said, "Not bad!" He was silent for a long pause. "I hope you're joking, the whole place is in a mess and you know it. It's got to be cleaned up. Tomorrow, you go underground to have a hard look at standards and workmanship and don't come back here and tell me that it's not bad."

I opened my mouth to say something but Smiley held up his hand.

"I know that standards are not your responsibility. They belong to the deputy and the oversman, but as Safety Officer you can help to achieve an improvement. I want you to put out a weekly bulletin on safety, work out on slogans, draw posters and get some films from area and show them in the Miners' Welfare. You know the stuff I'm after, you've done it all before."

The phone rang and Smiley picked it up. As he talked it gave me time to think about what I was supposed to do. Smiley put the phone down and drank some coffee.

"Now," he continued, "just bear with me until I am finished; then you can ask all the questions you want. The workmen here," he spread his hands as though they were in front of him, "they ride on conveyors, and on top of full mine cars; they leave their place of work early. It just goes on and on. It's not like any other pit you have worked in. They have had their own way so long that it will be difficult to change, but they must change, otherwise the pit will be closed down."

I continued to sit there, still silent, finishing off my coffee which was now cold.

"After saying all that," Smiley went on, "they are good miners, good in the sense of being efficient workmen."

Smiley was becoming a bit angry. "Why do they behave so badly, you may ask and the answer is because they get away with it." He paused for a moment and sat back in his chair. "They can call a strike, the union that is, and get a one hundred per cent turn out. They claim it has to be that way or otherwise it would be non-effective. Many a manager's confidence has been wrought out of him, but they won't break me."

He stopped and let what he had said sink in, giving me a chance to say something.

"Why didn't you give the Safety Officer's post to a local official?" I asked, "He would know the men and the layout"

"That's just the point," he replied. "It was a local man who had the post, but he had too many friends, and to do the job properly you can't afford to have too many friends."

A knock at the door interrupted Smiley, and his runner, George, popped his head round the door.

"Shall I set the Conference Room up for the Consultative Meeting?"

"Yes, and arrange for the tea with the canteen manageress."

"It's done," the runner said and was off again. George, Smiley's runner, 'his get', was a man in his early fifties who had been injured underground and deemed unfit for heavy work. Although he was in a position to pick up information from the manager's office and pass it on to the unions, he never did. The unions had long since stopped trying to compromise him, and he had the manager's trust.

Smiley was talking again. "I don't want you to rush into this, it will only upset the unions and make matters worse. No, take it easy, a bit at a time, settle in before you do anything drastic."

I was sitting taking all this in, wondering what I had I let myself in for. Surely, it couldn't be as bad as he was making out. I learned there was more to come.

"You won't be very popular here, as you don't belong. The pit is isolated, and all of the work force are local, including the officials. There are also a number of officials here who thought that they should get your job and you won't be loved by them either."

Smiley got up from his chair and walked to the window where he looked out at the yard. He said, "If I can pull this off, I may get the money to tarmac the yard. I'm sick of looking at that mess out there."

I had a feeling he wasn't talking to me, just thinking aloud. He turned and walked back to his chair, leaned forward on his desk and said, "Be alert to the unions, especially the N.U.M. They are very experienced in dealing with problems, and they are also capable of making holes for us to fall into. Stick to the law and don't land foul of them."

After a short pause, Smiley continued, "You will meet all these people today at the Consultative Meeting. I want you to attend."

We spent the rest of the morning chatting about old times then I was shown to my office, where I sat down and relaxed.

Here I am again, a new job, a new place and new faces, I was thinking. I seemed to be forever finding myself in that situation; seemed always to be moving to another pit, another boss, barely getting to know the people, then off again. It sure knocked hell out of friendships and caused a lot of grief in continually moving home.

When anyone arrives at a new place people stare at them and look them over. He is an intruder, and it will take a while for him to be accepted, but in time it will come and he'll settle down.

But for how long, I was wondering, as I sat there on that rainy day. One time, I recalled arriving at a new place, and apart from just one man, I was completely and utterly ignored.

That particular new place was a posting to my first active service squadron in Italy. I had travelled from North Africa and only the tiredness I felt was holding down my excitement, but even so it wasn't what I had expected. It was nearly dark when I arrived and was raining.

The squadron was housed in tents in a field, and everywhere underfoot was mud. I made my way along a narrow path made up of metal strips which followed a line down between the tents to a large marquee. This, I was to learn, housed the kitchen, dining room and bar.

The bar was full of half sloshed, unshaven flyers, with mud on their uniforms and short silk scarves around their necks and tucked into their tunics. The scarves were, I suppose, a gift from girl friends to be worn and to remember, and to show that they were flyers.

Every one had a glass in his hand and they were all laughing and gesturing. Their merriment filled the tent. I stood there taking in the scene, dressed, smartly, in R.A.F. blue with collar and tie. I must have looked odd, so clean and smart, the only black mark against me the mud on my shoes. Someone called me over to the bar, shook my hand and said "Welcome to the squadron."

Putting a glass of brandy in my hand, he added, "Blessed be the rain, long may it reign." We clicked glasses and drank. Then he turned away and I was on my own again. So this was an active service Squadron, this drunken scruffy bunch, the "Brylcream Boys." I was only eighteen and I had a lot to learn before I gave these men my greatest respect and admiration.

I was given a tent to sleep in, where the floor was laid with twigs and straw, and the bed was one of those metal strips which make up a runway. I lay down with my clothes on and with two blankets wrapped around me, listening to the rain falling on the tent. The brandy was taking effect and I soon fell into a sound sleep.

Next morning I was amazed at the state of the camp site - everything drenched in water and covered in mud. Apparently, it had been raining for three days and there had been no flying. It had stopped now, but the sky was still grey, 10/10 cloud, so, again, no flying.

I roused myself from my desk and my reverie and walked over to attend the meeting. The meeting. That was something else. I have known of smaller wars. It started off politely, as I was introduced, and then boiled over into a near revolution. I had ever experienced a meeting like that one and I was minute secretary to many meetings. Now, here I was taking the minutes of a fiasco.

The minutes of the previous meeting, having been handed out, were read and reluctantly passed, but not before the tradesmen's representative had complained that he had not been given a mention in them.

"My members, reading these minutes, will be thinking I wasn't at the meeting."

It was explained to him that the only matters recorded were those when a decision was taken or other matters that required to be looked into. From then on the meeting deteriorated.

I was to learn later that the National Union of Mineworkers, the (N.U.M), who had six members present, had held previous meetings in the Miners Welfare where each would take up an item on the agenda and then, at the Consultative Meeting, would play their hand out, one at a time, which was time consuming and time wasting. The officials put their two pence worth in only when they had to, being wise enough not to go too far. Smiley would patiently hear them out then call a halt when irrelevant topics were sneaked in.

"Stick to the agenda," he would say. "Don't come here to pull our little ranch to pieces bit by bit and expect me to build it up again. It's co-operation I want, constructive ideas and decisions taken, not just complaints."

The N.U.M. members sat smiling; they had achieved what they were after, to give nothing away and to get back as much as they could. The officials were silent, wishing they were somewhere else, and the tradesman's representative wishing the meeting was over and he could go for a pint in the Welfare. By this time, I'd stopped taking notes and looked toward Smiley. Shrugging his shoulders he leaned towards me.

*Expendable*

"Make up what you can" he said quietly, "and we'll make a minute out later."

From then on, I was to take the minutes of the Consultative Meetings, the Safety Committee Meetings and The Managers' Meetings with the Unions. I was soon to learn that I was to write a lot without saying anything.

It took me a few days to settle in and get my office in some kind of order. As for the pit, we would get a good output some days, but on others very little, mainly through breakdowns. Both chiefs complained that they hadn't enough men to deal with all their problems. The pit was very old, a new seam being opened up and most of the new plant coming into the pit was being deployed to this new seam. At the same time, trying to keep up production made a lot of demands on the chiefs.

Absenteeism was running at a high level, which included men off through sickness, accident and just plain absenteeism, especially when the salmon were on the run in the River Forth. The men were good at whipping salmon and making a handsome profit by selling them to the local hotels. They could make up to twenty pounds a day.

Our accident rate was no worse than any other mine, at about thirty a month, which may sound a bit high, but was mainly minor cuts and bruises which would keep a man off his work for only a couple of days. We were fortunate in having few reportable incidents. When a major bone is fractured or other serious injury happens, a Mines Inspector has to be called in to investigate the cause. If a fatal accident occurs the police may be called to the pit.

The pit was grinding away, grinding being the correct adjective, with trouble from the start of the morning: stuck conveyor belts, stuck A.F.C. chains, electric motors drowned out and attitudes bitter. Smiley began each day with his Monday morning face, straight, dour, strict, and showing no surrender.

His face shouted out at you, "Come within four feet of me and I will bite your head off."

By the time I saw him each morning he had usually softened a bit. I always got a 'Good Morning' from him, unless I was too early.

*Expendable*

Once, some years ago, I wished his Monday face a good morning, and he said. "Don't talk to me in the morning when there is no coal. Just put the report down and get out."

Okay, I thought, and so the next three mornings I laid the report in front of him without a word and with nothing from him either, I would leave. The fourth morning, as I laid the report under his nose, he grunted, which I suppose could have been a good morning. I said nothing and left the room, and as I was about to close door behind me he called me back.

"Haven't you got any manners?" and before I could answer he continued, "I said good morning to you."

I nodded and replied, "Good morning to you Mr. Smiley."

He laughed. The next day, he had his Tuesday face on. It's the same as Monday's but a bit more hopeful.

Smiley was in his early fifties, well built, with dark hair, dyed and thinning. It could be said of him that he was calm, patient and mainly tolerant. He could not stand fools gladly, was a straight no nonsense man,, who could stand a lot of pressure - which was inevitable as a Colliery Manager. I had known him at a previous colliery where he had been under manager. Now, he was the boss, tough, strict, but fair, and he had built up his own 'flying squad' of reliable men who could be called upon in difficult times to put things right. He paid them well. He was much of a loner and well respected.

Camdon was a difficult pit, geologically, and had a workforce with inborn practices, didn't make matters any easier. If you were not local you didn't belong, and neither Smiley nor I were local. At times the strain would show on Smiley when the men were acting up, when production was down, or the pit could not be manned properly because of absenteeism. When a workman was injured we always knew Smiley would arrive in the morning and, without a word, change into his pit clothes and vanish underground.

There was one incident that we all found amusing. The office cleaners would have his office ready for his arrival each morning along with the other offices. The office next to Smiley's had a coal fire and the cleaners would make up the fire and put the ash bucket outside Smiley's door. He didn't like that and had warned them to have it taken away before he arrived.

On this one morning they had forgotten and when he approached his office he saw the bucket full of ash. He swung his foot and gave it an almighty kick, hurling the bucket through the air to land in the middle of the yard. He stood there for a moment and watched it land, with a little smile on his face as though he was thinking that one problem had been solved. Then he turned and vanished into his office.

At other times, especially around Christmas, he would call to me to accompany him to the Miners' Welfare, where he was welcomed. He would walk about talking to the old retired miners offering each one a pint of beer and a glass of whisky. Even though we were mostly at loggerheads with the N.U.M. at the pit, when any of the staff ventured into their domain they were always welcomed. Although alcohol was never allowed at the pit, come the end of the year he gave a bottle of whisky to be shared amongst the staff.

There were times when the pit went well, production was up and maintained at a high level for weeks on end. Those were the good times, when meetings ran smoothly and everyone was in agreement. But it wasn't all for free. The N.U.M. made the most of any opportunities and would state, on occasion, that their men would give coal only at a price. An example of the price would be, effectively, a bribe: If a big football match was to be on the television, and the men on the afternoon shift wouldn't see it, the deal would be that they were to be allowed to go down the pit early and take over from the day shift at the coal face, keeping production going until they had obtained three complete shears. After that they would be allowed to go home or to the club to watch the match, without loss of wages.

What could Smiley say? What choice did he have? The alternative was that they would not turn up to work, so no coal would be produced. They had tried this bribery once before and Smiley had said no, with the result of a shift's production lost. So he agreed, but insisted that it must be done in an orderly manner. Nobody would be allowed up the pit in dribs and drabs, they must all come together and the oncost must stay at their workplace until the coal had been wound to the surface.

This was the sort of deal that had to be done with the N.UM. Committee, just to keep production up. It was sensible, you might think, but it was not the Coal Board's policy. A miner was supposed to go underground for a certain period of time, in this case seven and a half hours. He was there to produce coal and was paid accordingly, for any time shorter than seven and a half hours he would have his time docked. That was the policy. Even when a man was seriously injured or killed his time would be docked when he reached the surface. It was the same throughout the coal fields, but not at Camdon.

In the case where the Camdon men were let up the pit for a football match with three shears taken off the face, they were underground for only five hours, down at noon and up at five p.m. Fair enough, Smiley got his quota of coal and they all got their football match, but again this was dangerous territory we were working in.

"What of us?" the officials asked. "We also like to watch football."

"And us," called the tradesmen.

"I can't shut the pit down because of a bloody football match," snapped Smiley. "What will be next, a dinner dance or a trip to the sea side? No, you will all have to fall in line and get on with the job you get paid for."

That was the dilemma Smiley had to face up to, and any attempt on his part to bring normality into the system brought a response from the union, who would call for an overtime ban. No pit could operate successfully with an overtime ban hanging over its head. It was only at the weekend that repairs could be carried out, to have the coal face ready for production on Monday morning. Of course the union knew that, it was their way of playing by the book.

The N.U.M. Committee men were a very experienced lot, and they were led by a man called John Smart, a man of outstanding cunning and foresight. No matter how many castles we attempted to build, he could knock them all down if he had a mind to. If he co-

*Aircraft that I served in during the war*

*Brushers piece time*

*Roof collapse in heading injuring a workman*

*Repairers stabilising a roof which has been serverely crushed*

*Brushers setting a breaker to the roof to control the amount of debris being blown down*

*Setting a roof support at the coal face*

3

*Wood boys work on the coal face supplying the stripper with supports*

*Roof collapse at coal face on top of conveyor*

*Strippers at the coal face having their snack*

*Shot firer waiting for hole to be bored, to charge it and fire*

*Slack, slack, more slack*

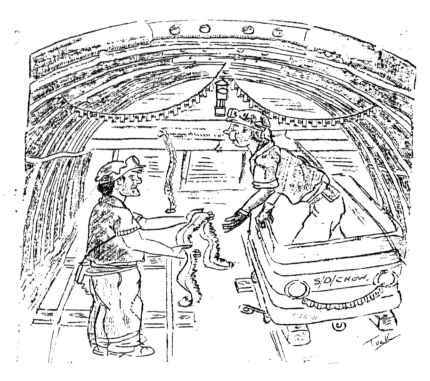

*It was the manager's idea*

*Jenny Gray Colliery, Lochgelly*

*Pumper*

*A road head incident*

*Developers*

8

operated with management you could depend on it that he would call in his tabs when the right time suited him. He could call a strike and get almost a hundred per cent turn out.

"A strike has got to be a hundred per cent, otherwise it is non effective," he would claim. He wasn't a man of large stature, on the contrary he was on the thin side, but wiry. He would fight with some of his members for not falling in line and he didn't always win.

Smiley was his old self this morning. He hated the world when in that mood. What had disturbed his peace of mind was an intended visit from the Head of Mines Rescue, as a previous visit had not ended amicably. After tea in the manager's office, the visitor claimed that he had come to inspect the new Rescue Room. Now that was something that we could be proud of. We had an excellent Rescue Room, fully equipped, and it pleased the Head no end. He actually left smiling, and for all of us it was nice to know that, sometimes, something good was said of Camdon.

Most of these tit bits are taken from my diary and there was so much happening in a day at Camdon that it was difficult to record everything, but here is an example:

*"The 'Shorok Alarm' people left yesterday but not before putting the alarm into operation without telling anyone; we were afraid to open the magazine."*

The next thing to happen occurred when an electrician, on night shift, was sent underground to do a job. He didn't go but, instead, he made himself comfortable in the winding engine room and went to sleep. He was found there by the chief electrician. Smiley sacked him of course, and then all the tradesmen walked out in support of their man. It was ridiculous. They wanted his job given back to him. It was going to be interesting to watch how this case developed, if the history of sacking at Camdon was anything to go by.

To me this was a serious dereliction of duty and the man ought to be punished. Should he have been offered his job back, it would have been for the sake of his wife and family because, ultimately, they are the ones who would be punished.

The action of this man and the other tradesmen was surprising to me as I found it hard to understand a man who would do this. He

*Expendable*

must have known that he would not get away with it and also the consequence if he were caught. A meeting was hastily called with the tradesmen's union, where they agreed to give emergency cover at the pit and put a ban on overtime thus allowing the pit to go on working in a fashion.

The next morning the Chief Electrician reported that someone had learnt to defeat the time delay in the main belt thruster brake. That caused a three and a half hour delay. At first it was thought to have been caused by a belt maintenance man, but after an investigation by the Deputy Chief Electrician the blame rested squarely on the tradesmen's shoulders. That being the case, matters were made even worse: That the machinery had been deliberately interfered with smacked as a mark of revenge for the sacking.

The next three hours were spent dealing with a young man suspected of having a spinal injury and he had to be handled with great care. We got him to the hospital with a police escort and the ambulance screaming along behind them. Those ambulance chaps could really lay it on with their siren. Luckily, the lad's spine was not damaged.

Matters didn't improve and the night shift went home on strike, a prediction Smiley had made earlier on account that the night shift 'Strike Leader', as we knew him, was a relation of the man who was sacked. The next morning, Smiley went underground and in a very short time six young men were sent back up the pit by him, their crime: long hair. It was the Board's policy that long hair must be kept tucked away in a hair net, and they had been issued with hair nets but young men wouldn't wear them, as it wasn't 'macho.'

Shortly after the young men came up the pit, I had the tradesmen's delegate and the N.U.M. delegate in my office, complaining of the manager's action. I made a telephone call to the store and was assured that hair nets were in stock and the lads could go to the stores and collect them. I couldn't help wondering why Smiley was laying the boot in, but I suppose it was his way of letting them know who the boss was.

Later that day, I noted an appointment in my diary for the following week. We were to attend a meeting, being held in

*Expendable*

Motherwell, to hear what Mr. Ezra, the Board's Chairman, and the top union officials had to say. There had been three disputes in twenty-four hours. That was not bad going, and I wondered if it had been planned that way, just a few days before such an important meeting. We didn't have much coal but we sure had strategy.

The next few days were hectic. I think that everybody who was a somebody called at the pit. They would have been informed, of course, about our continuing disputes. The Area Safety Engineer, Area Mechanical Engineer, and Electrical Engineer, The Production Manager, Deputy Director and many others all came to offer advice or help where they could, but I felt that it was mainly to ensure that none of the blame for the disputes would land on their shoulders.

Next, Smiley informed me that a Mr. McGomery was on his way to the pit. He was an N.U.M. Inspector, a good lad, a communist and a very humane person with a brilliant mind. I spent the rest of the day with McGomery and the N.U.M. Committee. He was there to inspect the installation of T.V. cameras on No. 4 Bank. The installation would allow us to wind coal up the pit without using a Banksman by skip. This would save a job, or as McGomery put it 'do a man out of a job.' Smiley had assured him that no man would be paid off.

The following morning found me underground, with Mr. Woods, H.M. Inspector of Mines, and Smiley. We were making our way into a production section, and as we approached the coal face, via the Main Gate, we were met by workmen running out, six of them. They were wearing their self rescuers and led by Smart the N.U.M. delegate.

Of course we were surprised, as Smart took off his self rescuer and claimed that there was an outbreak of fire in the top road, that the smoke was billowing down the face-line towards them. Smiley told him to stay where they were and we walked into the bottom of the face-line. The conveyor was still running and the rest of the workmen were working away, not wearing their self rescuers. Smiley stopped the conveyor and, looking around, he approached one man and asked him why if there was a fire in the top road he wasn't wearing his self rescuer?

The man was holding back a smile as he replied, "I didn't know that there was a fire."

Smiley, building up a head of steam, knew they were at it again. He shouted up the face-line, "Get the deputy down here right away!"

The deputy, who was on his way down the face-line was surprised initially, to learn that some of his men were wearing their self rescuers, but he wasn't surprised when he learned who they were. He explained that shots had been fired at the top end which had caused the smoke, and that there was no fire and no reason for the rescuers to be used.

"Get the section going again, I'm going to have a word with Smart and company." Smiley demanded. I could see that Smiley was fuming, and the Mines Inspector also noted Smiley's state.

"We had better take it easy," he suggested, "they may be genuine."

Smiley had forgotten the presence of the Mines Inspector, whose advice seemed to calm him down a little. Approaching Smart, he informed him that there was no fire and that they should get back to work. Smart, with a silly grin on his face, apologised for the commotion but still claimed that he thought there was a fire.

"O.K," Smiley said. "The fun is over, get back to work!"

"We can't go back to work, as we have used our self rescuers and so will have to return to the surface," Smart said, smugly.

Smart had had it all planned out. He knew we were coming, and that the Mines Inspector would back him for refusing to remain underground without a self rescuer. Later that day Smiley was still a bit angry over that fiasco but more concerned as to why Smart would pull such a stunt. He knew Smart to be wild but didn't think he would go to such lengths as he did and seemingly for no purpose.

It wasn't until later that he was to learn that Smart had had a row with the under manager that morning. Apparently, the under manager had refused him permission to get up the pit early and this was Smarts way of getting around the problem. Smart by name.

The next day production was brought to a standstill when the shearer undercarriage was broken again. All anyone could do was to wait until it had been fixed by the engineers. Smiley, with time on

*Expendable*

his hands, started to push me to complete the Safety Magazine, which I had been working on every spare minute. So I pushed the chief clerk to get it printed by the next week, but he said that he hadn't the time and that it should be left until the next month. I was not pleased, as I had run my feet off getting items together for the magazine and if it were left for a month the items would be out of date.

I spoke to Smiley, asking him to push the chief clerk a wee bit. He pushed a *big* bit, and was promised that the magazine would be out the next week.

I would have liked to have included in the magazine a report of the self rescuer fiasco, but I didn't think it would be right to broadcast such an item, as it would only cause embarrassment to the pit and also to Smiley. The N.U.M. were keeping a low profile about the whole matter.

Later that evening I was back at night school, where I was studying Higher English. The teacher was very young, pretty and patient, and the class was mainly manned by teenagers, including my son. They thought that I was a bit old to be studying with them and the teacher thought so too but after a while I was accepted as one of them. The teacher was on her favourite subject. Almost all the work she had given us up to now, poems by Yeats, Owen, Sassoon and Eliot, had been on the same subject – death.

At home, staying in to do homework, I finished a critical analysis of Edith Sitwell's play, '*Still Falls The Rain*.' I still had to do an essay on three poems on death. I was certain that our teacher was morbid. At this stage I had to give up, as the kids were making a racket and the television was on. I was not surprised at the noise because it was getting near to Christmas and we all know what that means. My son Philip wanted an airgun and he had been on about it continually for weeks. He asked me if I had a rifle in the air force.

"No," I told him. "I had a revolver, a 38 pistol."

Then I thought for a moment, and recalled that I did have a rifle at one time, while in the R.A.F, a German Mauser rifle, and then I told him a true story.

Our airfield was on the east coast of Italy, virtually right on a beach. The main beach for the town was over a mile away and very inviting. However, we were advised by our adjutant not to go there to swim as it could be dangerous. He warned us that the Italians, although defeated and apparently passive, were still the enemy and that there could be a number of snipers lying in wait. We didn't think that was likely, but never the less we took his advice and stayed at our own beach. But it was unsuitable for swimming, as it had little sand and was rocky. Anyway the weather was not that good for swimming.

Between bombing raids, we passed our leisure time sitting near the sea firing rifles. Quite a number of us had rifles, and we would shoot out to sea with whatever was available as a target. Our main target was a rowing boat anchored two hundred yards from the beach. We must eventually have shot it to pieces for, one day, we watched it slowly sink and disappear. I had a German Mauser rifle, but I stripped the wood off the barrel and turned it into a sports rifle. Why? Well, I liked the idea.

You may be wondering how we got hold of our rifles. We just picked them up here and there. There was no shortage of guns. The Italians were ordered to hand in all their weapons to the special military police and they got quite a collection, from the small Baretta to the German Luger, including a lot of rifles, so it was easy to acquire one. My problem was that I was running out of bullets for my Mauser.

I mentioned this to an army sergeant, who had come back from the front line to collect supplies and had stopped in at our mess for a meal and a drink. I also told him that I wanted a German steel helmet for flying. A lot of our flyers wore them on top of their flying helmets, after the insides had been removed. It was good protection for the head, especially for the gunners, as their heads protruded above the turret and were vulnerable to shrapnel strikes.

Anyway, the sergeant said that he would take me up to the front line which was only twenty miles away, to where I could get ammo and a helmet. I hadn't, until then, given much though to the front line. I had imagined soldiers lined up in trenches, lines and lines of them, but it was nothing like that. The front line was an imaginary line. As we drove up in the jeep, off the main road and across fields, I noticed that it was very quiet. Stopping the jeep, we climbed out and pointing to a notice by the side of a dirt track the sergeant said, "Read that notice."

I walked up to it and read, 'You are now under enemy observation.'

I was a bit shaken and asked, "What do we do?"

"Just follow me," he said dropping into a ditch beside a dirt track. Keeping his head down he quickly hurried to a farmhouse where the dirt track lead. He stopped short of the farmhouse and pointed to a shallow grave with a make shift cross stuck into the ground. On the cross was a German helmet. I looked again and saw the dead man's boots sticking out of the grave.

"Go on, get that one." I was advised.

I looked again, shuddered and answered weakly, "No, I couldn't take that one, it is his."

He gave me a look, smiled a little and without a word made his way, still crawling, to the farmhouse. We came up behind the farm house and to my great surprise, half a dozen British troops, in the forward position, were relaxed, sitting outside reading, one or two with their shirts off, taking in a bit sun. When I asked where the Germans were I was told about four or five hundred yards ahead. I suggested that if they were to attack then the soldiers would not be ready for them. Some of the men must have heard my worried voice. They just laughed and one of them brought me a cup of wine. The Sergeant said that the Germans wouldn't attack us at this time of the day, they were relaxed and doing what we were doing.

Explaining further, he said, "We go out on patrol when it is dark to see if the Germans are up to anything, and we pass the German patrol, who are looking to see if we are up to anything. We are not complaining. Here, have another cup of wine."

"What of snipers," I asked, "Won't they shoot at us?"

"They won't shoot at us, no more than we would shoot at them. As for snipers, they are only left behind a retreating army to slow down the advance. Here, there is no retreat and no advance, so no snipers."

*Expendable*

This was a bit too much for me, I collected some ammunition and a German helmet and, with my head a bit hazy, as I almost wept for that poor German with his boot sticking out of his grave, we made our way back to the airfield.

On arrival, I was to learn that all shooting had been stopped, as ordered by the Commanding Officer, and all rifles including mine, were to be confiscated. This was the result of the choice of target, by some clot, after we lost the rowing boat. There was little else to shoot at except, as he suggested, the meteorological balloon, sent up each day by the Americans, who had a squadron of Thunderbirds based at our airfield. He brought it down with his third round. Nothing was said about it, as far as we knew, until the next time we used their newly-replaced balloon, and again it was shot down.

Our actions this time almost started a war. The Yanks, already suspicious of the first balloon failure, were now certain of the cause of failure of their number two balloon. Not to be outdone, the Yanks shot down our met balloon. The situation escalated, at both ends of the airfield, where marksmen lined up and were ready to shoot down each other's balloons. Of course, this could not go on. Our C. O. gave orders for the guns and ammunition to be confiscated and he made a peace pact with the American Commanding Officer.

# CHAPTER NINE
## LAURENCE DAILEY

Three disputes in only twenty four hours, during the last week, and yet there we all were, strikers, unions and management, sitting together in a bus, chartered to take us to Motherwell, to meet Mr. Ezra, the Coal Board's chairman.

It was difficult to believe that these demanding, threatening and uncooperative men of last week were the same men we were sitting with today. They were all to a man, smartly dressed, talking politely with Smiley and his staff, as though they were the best of friends. The journey went off fairly smoothly, with no mention of the disputes. Smiley was quite content to leave the troubles behind at the pit and the unions must have had the same thoughts.

On route, Smiley pointed out to me the resting place of Lord Hamilton's ancestors. He told me that, years ago, the underground workings caused the monument to tilt slightly.

I felt sure that Lord Hamilton would have turned in his grave had he known what the miners had done to his proud stance. The bus journey continued, stopping outside the Civic Theatre. It was beautiful, if that is the proper adjective to use when describing a modern building.

As we approached the entrance a demonstration was being held back by police and security guards. The demonstrators, no doubt, were complaining about something or other. The communists were there in full force selling the Morning Star. The security was tight and I didn't think there would be any trouble, just that some people seemed to make a hobby out of demonstrating. May be some day we will see a demonstration against demonstrating.

On entering the theatre we were seated at the front row alongside the V.I.Ps. We had a grand view of the stage, where a long table had been set out to receive them. The speeches were started by the Board's Chairman, his theme being *'We Must Sell Our Coal.'*

He was good, very convincing, but of course that was to be

expected. Lawrence Dailey was on his feet next and also gave a good account of himself, followed by Patrick McGachey, with whom I can't always agree, but, still, he impressed me favourably. For once, he didn't try to start a revolution or, 'Bring down the Tories' but then that was to be expected considering the audience. Everyone at the top table who spoke kept politics and union demands unmentioned, and apparently, if the applause was anything to go by, every body agreed with the speakers.

After the speeches, refreshments were offered, whisky in particular, a refresher for some, but for the majority a tension remover, a knee softener, a tongue looser. I have never seen so much free drink given out, ever, and by far it would outstrip any New Year Party. There were no abstainers.

I met many old friends from pits I had previously worked in; they were there from all over the mining community. Laurence Dailey, standing with a whisky in his hand, called me over to join him. We were old friends from the past and spoke together for fifteen minutes. He told me that my drawings of years ago were in the archives in London, drawings that I had produced to illustrate a magazine we were working on together called *Pit Bits*. During our talk many approaches were made to him but he just put them off by saying that he was in the middle of a discussion. Me, I was fair chuffed.

When it was time to go home, most of our party were well on the way, and I was being continually questioned by them as to my acquaintance with Dailey. They were surprised and a bit envious, I was pleased to note. Smiley was also curious. I told him that Dailey and I at one time worked at the same pit, where he was the N.U.M. delegate and I worked on development.

"Dailey was producing a magazine and I drew the illustrations and cartoons," I explained. "I was a budding artist at the time, drawing cartoons for a couple of newspapers and Dailey knew this and asked me to help."

"Was he a communist then," asked Smiley.

"Oh, yes," I replied, "and his father, I believe, was also a communist."

"What about you, were you in the Party?"

"No, I was not politically minded."

"But you subscribed to the communist propaganda?"

"I never looked at it in that way, I was just a young man looking for recognition."

"He came up from the roots then?' Smiley asked.

"Yes and he had a good following, I can remember that on a Saturday night when the only thing in our minds was beer, he could be seen at Lochgelly Cross, standing on a wooden chair addressing a group of men on their rights. Rights that they weren't allowed to have."

Smiley was silent as though waiting for me to continue. Well, that wasn't difficult, as I had indulged in some tongue loosener.

"Miners in general don't get involved in politics; it makes no difference to them who is in power as they still have to go down the pit each day, and their drudgery won't get any less. Although I can't go along with what Dailey says, I do believe he is sincere in his beliefs, and had he been in with Labour or Tory or Liberal at that period of time, he would have been up in Parliament."

"He must have known what the possibilities were yet he still remained a Communist," Smiley remarked, after a moment's thought.

I agreed, then added, "If you remember the Russian invasion of Hungary, it was then rumoured that Laurence had left the Party. I asked him about the rumour, and he said that he was still a communist but not a Russian type, as he didn't agree with what the Russians had done."

It was becoming difficult by now to hear ourselves speak as our party in the bus were having a sing song, so we just sat back and listened to them.

It was some fifty years later, while on a visit to Fife to see my younger sister Jean, that she announced she had a surprise in store for me. She handed me four copies of our old magazine *Pit Bits,* the same magazine that. Dailey had told me about in Motherwell. I was delighted, amazed, I couldn't believe it, the same magazine I had drawn cartoons for all those years ago. That should floor the critics who didn't believe what I was doing back then.

Jean told me that she had obtained the magazines from the local councillor named William Hamilton who knew that I was visiting Fife and thought that it would bring back memories, especially the cartoons. I knew William Hamilton from away back. He was only a child then, still at school, and lived next door to us. The day I shot the crow down our neighbour's chimney, he was one of the kids who ran out of the house in a cloud of soot. I wonder if he can remember the incident. Anyway thanks for the magazines, Willie.

Reading through the magazine much later I remembered the old troubles in the pits. The magazine was produced by the N.U.M. committee of Glencraig Colliery, which was made up mainly of Communists, and contained a lot of communist propaganda within its pages. Reading it even now you could sympathise with them in their efforts. It made a lot of sense then.

They fought for wages and conditions and the welfare of the mining community. Miners, at this period of time, were not particularly militant and were not all members of the union. Of the one thousand and forty one miners employed at the colliery, only nine hundred or so were members, which was a sore point with the union. The reason, I suppose, was that communism was not very popular in the country at that time. This was in the 1940s with wages very low.

When I started in the pit as a surface worker, I earned less than a pound a week, three shillings a day, which in today's rate would be fifteen pence. By 1950, a young man's wage was seven shillings a shift, or thirty five pence in today's money. Underground he would receive fifteen shillings, about seventy five pence, so in a way the union committee could hardly be blamed for their communist ideals.

Of course it wasn't all propaganda, but they did push it a bit. In those magazines was one bit that I don't understand.

"People in communist countries are better off than you," they claimed.

If that was the case then why were they having collections to send off to the poor miners of these other countries? Asking us for help when we were only getting fifteen pence a day was not on.

There were articles on sport, reports of the local football team's progress, even poetry and, of course, the cartoons which I drew.

The cartoons, primitive by today's standards, were drawn on stencil paper with a stencil pen, that is a waxed sheet with lines and holes scratched on to it with a pointed stencil pen and you never knew the result of your work until a copy was produced. I have included a few of the cartoons so you can see what I mean.

There is a piece of history recorded in the magazine which I think could be of interest to the older miner. It was when the Coal Industry was being nationalised and refers to the payments to the previous owners made in 1947 and 1948. Apparently, a Bill was going through Parliament which would give them further interim payment in 1949.

William Gallagher, M.P. for West Fife, the only communist in Parliament, made the following statement during the debate.

"We have a situation in this country under the Labour Government in which, as a result of these interim payments, which were made last year, and the interim payments which are made this year, the mine owners of this country, including the honourable gentlemen opposite, are already better off under nationalisation than they would have been if they still owned their semi-bankrupt industry. I ask the Minister to consider, once again, whether he should go ahead with the Bill.

I am certain that he could make a gesture which would arouse the strongest possible support of the miners of the country and give a terrific impetus to coal production if he would stand up at the box, get the Bill, tear it into pieces and throw it into the wastepaper basket."

Of course, William Gallagher was known as the 'Miners' Champion' and is well remembered as such. Here also was Laurence Dailey, who featured a lot in the production of the magazine, which proudly quoted his rise from his low beginning in Glencraig Rows to becoming the General Secretary of the National Union of Mine Workers, no mean achievement. Glencraig Colliery was, I believe, one of the few pits that produced a magazine for the miners.

But to get back to the pit, as if you could get away from it. It had

*Expendable*

been raining heavily all night and when I arrived at the pit it was still pouring. The yard was in a mess. It was late February, the worst month of the year and it was dark, dreary and depressing

An old Scottish word describes the situation best, *dreich* meaning miserable. The night shift deputy had come up from underground, but his relief had not turned up, so it was to me and Smiley that he reported that two of the three turbine pumps had packed in and the water was rising up the dook.

There was more bad news. Only two pumpers had turned up for work. It was the weekend, when all maintenance is done, but none was to be done this weekend as the overtime ban by the tradesmen and N.U.M. was still on. Smiley shook his head in disbelief. We ran around all day trying to get the unions to allow men to work on the pumps. Otherwise the pumps would have been drowned out. Finally, we were successful, but what a day it had been, and it was still raining.

That evening, back at night school, I got another 'A' for my critical analysis. I did the 1972 English exam paper on interpretation and language. I'd got the subject off by pat, but the marker didn't think so. I got top marks for homework and came out bottom on the exam papers. I had got to the stage with Higher English where I didn't care whether I passed or not, but I intended to keep at it for my son's sake as I had promised that if he went back to college, then, I would stick it out with him, and he had agreed.

It meant two nights a week were committed, as I had also enrolled in the Higher Arts class. Raymond had been at college for two years, and didn't take it seriously. He fooled around, and didn't study much, so he didn't make the grade.

Back at the pit the following week, I was told that I had been given an assistant called Eddie Gray. He was to work with me and help out the other members of our team where required. At first sight he appeared confident, jaunty and friendly, but later we were to find that he was very unreliable and needed a lot of supervision.

When we got him to work he was good, very experienced in mining skills, an all rounder, but he would rather skive on the surface than get involved underground. He had a talent for remembering stories and would keep us laughing.

Smiley advised me that Mr. Woods, the Mines Inspector, would visit the pit on night shift and that I was to go with him. We thought that he would be checking our stone dust barriers which are shelves hung from the roof loaded with fine stone dust in the return side of a coal producing section. Their purpose was to act as a stopper should there be a gas ignition on the coal-face. The blast of the explosion knocks the shelves over and fills the air with stone dust, hopefully in greater quantities than coal dust.

It is known that coal dust can ignite and cause an explosion of greater force than a gas explosion. Stone dust, in excess, damped down this effect and was also required to be spread around in all return airways leading from the coal-face, to get the proper mix of coal dust and stone dust to prevent an explosion.

Smiley was off to Edinburgh to meet the new Director. He was probably about to get his bum skelped for his production, or rather for the lack of it. There was to be a special meeting on Thursday about the tradesmen's strike. I hoped that they would decide to return to work, but I didn't think so. I went over the magazine security system. Security, everybody knows how it works.

I went home to get some sleep and Eddie went under ground with the Ventilation Officer to check on the dust barriers and dusting in general. However, they didn't make it, and when I returned to the pit later they said that the man-rider had broken down and they had come back up the pit.

"Well," I thought, "if my guess is right, and Mr Woods is after dust barriers, someone else is going to get their bum skelped."

I had got up from my bed at seven p.m. and waited as the clock pushed me nearer to night shift. Philip had made telephone calls to girls, George's school report informed me that he was lazy, just like the rest of them. Sometimes I thought that Ruth and I had created a rest home and that we were the workers.

I got to the pit at eleven and Mr Woods was already there. He told me he had come to inspect the dust barriers and roadway dust.

"I knew it." I thought. "The Ventilation Officer will take a fit, he was dreading this."

*Expendable*

Heading back up the pit, to the canteen for tea and bread rolls, Mr. Woods and I had an interesting discussion, we even spoke of religion, and he surprised me when he asked if Catholics had the same Christ as Protestants.

I wondered if he was having me on. Before I left for home I made out a written report for Smiley and a note for the Ventilation Officer and Eddie advising them to take to the hills.

The chiefs, C.C.E.E. and C.C.M.E. were spending a lot of time at the pit as the tradesmen were allowing only emergency cover. I had come to the conclusion that most of the work force thought there would be an all-out strike. Another pit meeting had ended and the bottom line was 'Get back to work or else.' Back home, I tried to read up on *Pride and Prejudice*. I managed to read five chapters, but didn't take it in very well, and the book, I was sure, would feature in our exam.

At the pit the next day, Smiley was on to me about the safety magazine, and he then reminded me that I had a film show to put on at the Miners' Welfare on Sunday.

He asked, "What films do you have."

"I haven't got any yet. I haven't had much time to make arrangements."

"Just stop what you are doing and get the films," he ordered.

I pushed a wee bit and said, "I am trying to finish off the minutes of the last safety meeting."

"They can wait. Get the films," he said again.

Leaving his office, I got hold of Eddie and sent him off to the film library and told him not to return without a strip film. He was successful in his mission, so I could now guarantee a full house on Sunday.

It's marvellous when you consider what had to be done to get the safety message across. We provided free beer and a sex show so that I could get the opportunity to talk to the workmen about their own safety. The craftsmen still had the pit on emergency cover and I was hoping that the Sunday show would put them in a better frame of mind and get everything back to normal. Huh! This *is* normal for Camdon.

The Sunday film show was a great success. I had expected a full house, or at least a good turn out, as word got around about free beer and a sex film. What more could a man want?

I showed a couple of films on Accident Prevention, then gave a short talk on the increase in the accident rate at the colliery, showing charts on accident statistics which only the Safety Committee would normally see. The free beer was Smiley's idea. He looked at gatherings from a different angle, apart from safety. He maintained that giving free beer spread the money around, the money which the colliery had won in safety competitions. He would say it was the fairest way of ensuring that the men got a share in the winnings

Anyway, I got a good hearing and a fair round of applause, but was not sure if the applause was for my short talk, or that they were glad it had finished, and I was inclined to believe the latter, especially in view of what was about to take place next. First the film, and then a Go Go Girl. I had taken Eddie along with me to assist with the equipment and he had suggested that we accept the Club Committee's invitation to stay and watch their show. I did accept and their show started off with a girl singer, who was terrific. Then on came the Go Go Girl, and she was great also.

We had been given seats at the front of the stage and obviously, Eddie and I had been pointed out to the girl. She did her act, half on stage and the other half on Eddie's knee but he didn't mind, he said he enjoyed it, and I believed him.

# CHAPTER TEN
## STRIKE

The Tradesmen's Union had always been a bit uncooperative with management, and we felt that this was mainly due to the National Union of Mineworkers' apparent hold on all union matters at the pit. The Tradesmen's Union was left to play second fiddle, except when the N.U.M. said differently, resulting in, among other things, animosity and envy. Their non-co-operation with management was their way of gaining credibility and status.

Of the four unions at the pit N.A.C.O.D.S; S.C.E.B.T.A; N.U.M; and C.O.S.A, none would co-operate with any other. A mask of friendship was worn to hide the hostility, and under these circumstances it was little wonder that the pit was on the brink of strike action all the time.

Management was not surprised when acts of vandalism began to happen with the sole purpose of stopping production of coal. Some of the vandalism could quite easily have been called sabotage, a serious crime which could carry penalties including a loss of job from the pit and other industries, plus a term in jail. It was becoming obvious to management that the person doing this, knowing the great risks they were taking, must have been a bit short in grey matter.

For example, the dust control water system for the shearer, which in some mines would run for a few miles or coal cutter, was supplied all the way from the surface. All along this water column, positioned at intervals, were shut off valves. These valves were being closed by someone, thus preventing the water from reaching the shearer and causing it to be stopped. A lot of time, as well as production, was lost until the guilty valve was found and the water restored.

Another production stopper was much more devious and nasty. Not only did the culprits commit the sabotage but they covered up the evidence so that it would not be easily found. The armoured face conveyor ran the whole length of the coal face, approximately two hundred yards, and had an excellent emergency stop system installed at intervals along the conveyor. Basically, it was a push button stop switch and, when operated, a light came on to indicate the point where the conveyor had been stopped. That was fine, but the culprit also covered the light with mud so that it could not easily be found. You can well imagine the time lost to production before the offending switch was found.

On the Monday morning I got back to the colliery and went to report to Smiley. He asked how the show had gone and asked if I got any inclination from the men as to their feelings about the strike. I told him of the meeting which had been held by the Unions before the show at the Welfare. He knew of that already so I told him that when I inquired as to the possibility of a return to work, or a strike, I was told to wait and see.

We both knew what that meant. There would be a strike. Everybody expected one. The Chiefs complained that without their men they could not hold out much longer, mainly because there hadn't been any progress since the sacking of the electrician who had fallen asleep. We all felt that the Tradesmen's Union was about to do something drastic, and that night I was informed by phone that there would be a strike on Monday morning.

The Tradesmen's Union had indeed done something drastic. They had voted for an all-out strike at the meeting on Sunday morning. They also threatened to withdraw the winding engine men but had held back on the advice of the N.U.M. who told them that to take such an action was madness.

The pit would close down as no one would get underground to prevent a flood. On Monday morning, the union held a special meeting of their members to take stock of the situation, and they also had discussions with the Craftsmen's Union, but it came to nothing. The winding engine men were withdrawn at the end of the day shift after every man had returned to the surface.

Smiley was forced to send all the N.U.M. men home. They had come prepared to work only to be told that there was no work for them. A row had developed into a major confrontation where nobody would win and, as usual, it would be the workers who lost most. The deputies were hanging about in the report room while a meeting with the Chiefs was going on in Smiley's office. The outcome was that the Chief Engineer would operate the winding engine to allow the deputies to go underground and carry out their inspections.

This idea did not go down at all well with the deputies. They were uncertain of the Chief's abilities as an operator, but it was finally agreed that only three deputies would go underground, each shift, and the remainder would go home.

The next thing to happen was that the deputies refused to operate the main pump, so we were no better off. The pit would still flood. The deputies maintained that they were not allowed to operate N.U.M. manned pumps. Smiley sent for the N.U.M. Committee and asked them to allow pumpers to work. They refused, but agreed to allow a member of staff to keep the main pump going. The member of staff chosen, of course, was yours truly. In one instance I went underground to the main pump at noon and did not return to the surface until seven the following morning. I should have been relieved by Eddie, but he took cold feet and stayed at home.

All that week there was an endless stream of meetings but no progress. The Tradesmen's Union was very much in the wrong over this issue. It was their man who went to sleep on the job, they who put on an overtime ban, called an all-out strike and withdrew the winding engine men. We all realised that they must return to work before negotiations could take place, which they must also have undoubtedly known. It began to seem that the bosses of the Tradesmen's Union, at national level, would be required to put pressure on them, to make them see sense and order their men back to work. Only then would they be able to get round the table and get this dispute sorted out.

In the end it was all sorted out by pressure from the top, but a compromise had to be made. The man who started the trouble got his job back, but not at Camdon. He was given a job at the area workshops and left after a short time to join up with an electrical firm. Looking back, it was all so silly and left a few red faces, as well as mistrust amongst the unions.

Nobody was sorry that it was all over and, as some put it, it was a welcome break. The ironic thing about it was that my accident rate was rising and yet there were no men at the pit. I put it down to an attempt to make up lost earnings.

Camdon Colliery was, in a way, unique. Where most pits had two shafts, Camdon had three. Shafts one and two were downcast, where as the third shaft was an upcast. No. 1 shaft was mainly for men, No. 2 was a skip wind for coal, No. 3 was used to transport heavy and awkward material underground, and was sunk, along with No. 1, much deeper to the old workings, which were now abandoned. It was now used as a pumping station and required to be inspected regularly by the Ventilation Officer, and that's where this story begins.

The Ventilation Officer, on one of his inspections to the old workings, reported that black damp was seeping out of an old roadway, and Smilcy decided to have the offending road closed off. A stopping would have to be built which might create a few problems. To put you into the picture, no workmen were allowed into this part of the colliery unless supervised, as the roadways weren't all that secure. The timbers behind the circle arch girders were so rotten, that you could literally push your finger through them. Then there was the black damp. As you probably know, black damp is contained in an atmosphere where there is no oxygen, its specific gravity makes it heavier than air and thus it lies on the floor and it can be fatal.

It was arranged that the Ventilation Officer, Eddie, four workmen and me, of course, would go down and do the job. A deputy or oversman would normally have been present also as all workings, and roadways, must be covered by a deputy's district, but all three of us were qualified as deputies, and the manager could appoint any one of us as in charge of that part of the mine. Anyway, the deputies had no quarrel with that, being quite happy to leave it to us as there were other problems associated with having to go down this shaft, black damp for instance.

It all depended on the barometer. If there was a high in air pressure we could go down, if there was a low, no way. But it was not left entirely to the barometer. Before anyone was allowed to go down to the old workings a flame safety lamp was hung on the cage and the cage would be lowered to the bottom. The cage was left in the bottom for five minutes before being brought to the surface and then, if the lamp was still lit, we could go down, but if it was out, black damp was present and we would wait for a high barometer.

We sent a lamp down and it came up still lit, so we went down. I should explain that two thirds of the shaft's depth was the normal landing to the workings, and the remaining third where we were going, was to the old workings. Getting off the cage at the old bottom, I led the way, with my flame lamp down by my side, the ventilation officer next with the four workmen and Eddie coming up in the rear. There was a stillness about the place, which was dark and damp; the air smelled of decay and there were cotton balls of white fungus hanging from the roof. We were only a short way in when Eddie called that his lamp had gone out. The V. O. immediately raised his lamp a bit higher and called back, "It's O. K. The gas is on the floor and we are stirring it up with our feet as we walk in."

One of the young men said that he could smell it and then added, "And I can taste it."

When we reached the place where the stopping had to be built, we sat down to have a snack and noticed that the two young men were not at all happy with the situation. The V. O. was doing his best to reassure them that all was well and that there was no real danger.

He said, "I do this all the time, don't worry. I'm no hero, if it was bad I would be up the pit like a shot."

The two older men had no problem with the situation, and were keen to make a start. The two young men would gather the stones that lay about and lay them to the side of the stopping at hand for the builders. Meanwhile, the V. O. went off to do his usual inspection leaving Eddie and me to look after the men. I'd asked him if he wanted one of us to go with him but, shaking his head, he said, "I won't be long."

His inspection would take him on a roundabout road to the bottom of No.1 shaft, where a pump was positioned, and I reckoned that it would take him a good twenty minutes or so. Eddie's job was to go back to the bottom and phone the winding engine man every half hour to report that all was well, and between phone calls he would give the young men a hand to gather rubble.

Smiley had advised me not to keep the men down the pit too long, about four or five hours would be enough. The men knew of this and agreed to work on and go to the surface for their piece. That was fine, it suited us.

The Ventilation Officer's time was up and he hadn't returned and Eddie was getting a wee bit worried, but I reassured him.

"The V.O. knows this place like the back of his hand. We'll give him another ten minutes. He'll be all right, I promise."

The V. O. was a man in his fifties, very sensible, and who had been in mining all his days. He had probably come up against a problem and was dealing with it.

"Any way," I said, "I'll go and look for him just in case he needs a help with something."

I went off, leaving Eddie with the men and took the road that I knew the V.O. would have taken, as I had been with him before. There was no longer any crush on the roadway as the roof had settled a long time ago but I encountered a number of small falls of roof.

The whole place was creepy, still smelling of decay, and feeling the dampness on my face, unsettling thoughts began to enter my mind: it was like walking through a tomb and starting to imagine things.

Would I find the V. O. under a pile of rubble? Would he have fallen down a sump?Of course, I didn't believe it, and put the thoughts out of my mind as soon as they entered, but it was unsettling. I walked on, keeping my eye on my safety lamp and then, as I turned, the last bend, I found him.

He was standing near the bottom of No. 1 shaft at the edge of a large pool of water. Noticing my light, he turned to face me, and as I walked up to him I could see that he was frowning.

"The pump is not taking the water, the suction end must be stuck up with mud or something," he said.

I looked around, taking stock of the situation and put my hand on the pump.

*Expendable*


"It's heating up," the V. O. said, "That's why I think the suction is partially blocked."

The bottom of the shaft was about twenty feet away and the water at that point some four to five feet deep. The area was high and wide with little support, and was cut out of solid rock. Nevertheless, it still looked wild, scary, with water dropping down the shaft and splashing about everywhere.

The V.O. was speaking again.

"When things are normal I can walk up to the suction and clean it, now I'll need a snorkel."

"If I gave you a hand, do you think we could pull it out?"

We tried, but it wouldn't come. Planting our feet firmly, we tried again, and on the count of three we gave an extra effort and pulled. The V.O. staggered, slipped and went under. I let go of the hose bag and grabbed for his hand, which was searching above the water to get a hold of something. Pulling him to his feet, with water running from his clothes, he wiped his eyes clear whilst still holding on to me. His helmet was in the water and his lamp had gone out. It shouldn't have gone out, but it did. Picking his helmet out of the water I examined his lamp. The glass was cracked.

As we stood there I looked at him, and he was actually grinning. He looked silly, standing there, soaked through like a drookit duck and grinning. I just grinned back and we both burst out laughing as we waded out of the water. He couldn't carry on now that he was wet through. We were at the bottom of No.1 Shaft, a downcast shaft which was very cold. He would have to go to the surface, so we made our way back round the circuit and met up with the others.

"Are you alright?" Eddie asked, as we approached our group

It's funny, why do people always ask if you are alright, when you are obviously not. You could be lying with a broken leg and as sure as reek goes up the lum, someone will ask the same question. It would probably be the same if you had just been shot or pulled out from under a roof fall.

Anyway, the V.0. went up the pit with the two young men and I took Eddie and the two workmen back to the bottom of No.1 shaft, thinking that the four of us should be able to pull the suction bag clear and get the pump started. Walking into the water in single file, with me in front, of course, we all got hold of the hose bag and on a signal, gave an almighty pull. The hose came clear, suddenly; we all staggered back and I went under, suffering the same fate as the V.O.

This time I was not laughing, nor as far as I could see, were any of the others, at least not until my back was to them. With the suction end cleared and put back in the water, we started the pump, waited a few minutes to see that it was taking the water, then off we went, hurrying up the pit. As I waddled towards the pit head baths I met the V.O. coming out. He was washed and dressed and stared at me with a smirk on his face. I'm not laughing, the look on my face told him, but as I moved away into the baths I'm sure I heard a peal of laughter behind me.

Smiley was getting ready to go on a course to Harrogate and so the under manager was to be in charge. He was taking notes of what Smiley was advising him.

"What ever you do, don't make matters worse," Smiley said.

The under manager, who up to this point been silent, remarked, "The way things are, they couldn't get any worse."

I was told that I had to arrange for a photographer to come to the pit to get a picture of the crush in the main gate of a production section. Because the weight of the roof and sides of the roadway was excessive, the support girders were being severely crushed, which was not normal. It was thought that we had a bad batch of steel. The picture would be picked up by an Area Official called Mr. Ludin. Eddie, my helper, was a member of the N.U.M. and Dave Wilson, the Chairman of the N.U.M. Committee had advised me that Eddie as a union man, would have to toe the N.U.M. line, which was to comply with their rules. In this instance, that meant a ban on overtime.

That was just great. Most of our work underground, such as advancing dust barriers, stone dusting the roadways, and checking clearances for locomotives and haulages, was done at weekends. Eddie also assisted me, first thing in the morning, in reading and preparing the deputies' reports for Smiley. That didn't go down well with the deputies and they complained to Smiley, objecting to a

N.U.M. man reading their reports. The only way I could see around this problem was to get Eddie into C.O.S.A, the staff association. union. C.O.S.A. was as much use to us as castor oil is to a cow, so joining would effectively mean that he would be free of the unions. C.O.S.A. was the smallest union at the colliery, whose members were employed mainly on a supervisory capacity and worked closely with the manager.

This left them with little clout where disputes were concerned. There were only a handful of their members at the colliery compared with the N.U.M. who were the largest union. There were also some N.A.C.O.D's members (officials), and lastly S.C.E.B.T.A. members (tradesmen) . They don't have a common goal.

The oversmen and deputies were in charge under ground. The deputy, where there is no oversman, was overall in charge of a district, including coal production, transport systems and all other work within the confines of his district. He was responsible for his men's safety, and this included tradesmen.

The under manager was in charge of all operations underground and reported directly to the manager. It was a system that worked most of the time, but relations could become a bit strained when, for whatever reason, coal was not forthcoming. Then, the pressure was put upon those responsible for the lack of production, and it was not done in a way that helped relations.

It was not a polite, "I say, old man, do you think you can possibly arrange to give us some coal today?"

The pressure was passed right down the line from the Director to the Production Manager, to the Colliery Manager, to the under-manager and on to the deputy, ending up at the coal face.

There were many things that could go wrong to stop production and a man's hand was in most of them. Whether accidentally or intentionally, the result was the same. No coal.

Smiley went off to Harrogate and the Under Manager was in charge. We were getting coal up the pit a lot better than of late. The next day, seven men, who had been transferred to us from another colliery, came up the pit on dispute. They wanted to be paid more than the National Agreement rate, which was ninety per cent of their previous wage. They were of the opinion that they were entitled to the full one hundred per cent and that all they would have to do was to present themselves at the pit and the money would be theirs. They wanted top wages even though they were not holding down top jobs.

During the week that Smiley was away, broken A.F.C. chains put a stop to our hopes that we could achieve output target which was, I believe, three tons per man, totalling at a minimum three thousand tons. The A.F.C. chains should have been the last thing to separate, and yet we at Camdon seemed to have more separations that any other colliery in the area. This could only have been because of poor maintenance, poor supervision, or an act of sabotage, perhaps all three. Five days later, the pit was still at a standstill and the cause was more broken chains.

The day Smiley was due to arrive back from Harrogate, I was to meet him at the airport. The under manager had briefed me on what to report to him, because we knew the first thing Smiley would ask. I had been advised to tell him that the week had been a disaster. We had managed to produce the target output on only a single shift. There had been no delays, we just churned out coal, and it seemed, for that one period, that the under manager was going to produce the goods in Smiley's absence, but his glory was short lived, and the pit never produced for the rest of that week.

Smiley was nowhere to be seen at the airport, so I telephoned his wife to inform her. I told her that the next flight would be much later and that I would return to the airport to meet it. I had just arrived home when Mrs. Smiley phoned to say that her husband was at the airport waiting for me.

"He is a wee bit upset, in fact, he is angry." She sounded a bit upset herself. "In fact, he is very angry."

I picked him up half an hour later. He opened the car door and immediately asked about the pit, so I told him what he wanted to know. He made no comment. Then, on the way home, he told me that he had a good week at Harrogate and seemed very relaxed.

He had been glad to get away from the pit, I thought. He smiled and said that he might have offended his wife on the telephone. I smiled back, thinking that Smiley could offend a saint without putting his mind to it. I spent most of the next day with the First Aid Team, or at least with those that attended. We were supposed to be preparing for our competition entry but not enough people turned up to make up a team. It was ridiculous. We had forty officials at the pit, all qualified and experienced first aiders, and yet to get a team of five seemed impossible, and with the competition only weeks away.

Smiley had brought his old moody self back with him. The pit was standing again, more chain trouble.

The photographer called at the pit and I took him underground to the troubled area. We walked for miles, carrying a ridiculously heavy flasher unit that didn't work when required. The coal face was standing when we arrived and, yes, you guessed it, the problem was chain trouble. The main gate was full of men, hanging about waiting for repairs to be made. I informed them that the roadway would require to be stone dusted. As the flasher unit didn't work, it was necessary to whiten the area with the dust, so that the pictures could be taken. The real reason was that, had I allowed the photos to be taken of the roadway when it was looking as black as a pit, then I would have deserved to be shot.

Stone dusting is never done where men are at work, and rightly so, as the workmen swallow enough coal dust without having to put up with stone dust as well, so I was on a sticky wicket here. A bribe was required before the men would agree to allow the stone dust to be laid. I had to promise we would take a picture of the whole group, which we did. The picture should have been published in the police gazette. The business at hand being completed, I suggested that we use up the rest of the film with some pictures that might be of use to Smiley. At least they would compensate for the group photo. God only knows what he would say when he saw it. I'd have to get a good story ready.

On the way back up the pit we arrived at the man rider at the bottom of the dook at about half past twelve. Whilst we stood waiting, and within a very short time, the face-men were out behind us. Obviously they had left their place of work much too early. They should have had their time docked, but what could you do, when the officials were out with them?

*Expendable*

Arriving at the surface, Mr. Ludin was waiting for us. He wanted to know if everything went okay regarding the photographs. He also said that the photos were to be sent to him. He would scrutinise them after they were developed, and we would only receive the ones which he felt were suitable. Smiley was annoyed at this arrangement and I wasn't too pleased either; I was thinking of the group photo and some others.

I slipped off, making an excuse, and headed for the canteen where the camera crew was having a spot of lunch. They were all good lads and when I told them of Mr. Ludin's arrangements they agreed to send only the official photos to him and the rest to us at the pit. Before he left the colliery, Mr. Ludin asked Smiley to give him a few flame safety lamps, the spare ones he said. Smiley assured him that we didn't have any spares, that all our lamps were needed. Ludin was not pleased, as he knew that we would have quite a few spares, as all pits have, but Smiley stuck to his guns and denied any knowledge of spares.

However, Ludin did get away with one lamp, but we still took pleasure in the deception, which was our way of getting even with him for being highhanded about the photos.

# CHAPTER ELEVEN
## EMBARRASSING MOMENTS

When I got home, my wife suggested that after a spot of lunch we should all go to the camping exhibition at Edinburgh. I did not argue, as it would be nice to think about holidays. We were great campers, having camped all over the country in previous years and often at weekends. We had to, because we had too many children to afford holidays in a hotel or boarding house.

Up to now I have not said much about my family and they are part of the story, part of my life, and should be included. I got married after I had left the R.A.F. My wife's name was Ruth and she was the youngest of a family of ten. Over the next few years we had five children, Christine the eldest, then Raymond, whom we managed to send to college, and Philip, Steven and young Ruth who was named after her mother.

We then 'adopted' three more. My brother and his wife had divorced so we took his son George and fostered two young brothers, Derek and Allan, whose parents had also divorced. That made a grand total of eight children. At the time of writing they are all married and have children of their own. As it stands at the moment we are the proud grand parents of fifteen grand children and four great grand children.

Anyway, camping is freedom. You just pack the car, drive to the end of the street, flip a coin to decide which direction, right or left, and off you go. We had a good knowledge of camp sites within three hundred miles from our home, sometimes we would camp outwith a campsite, beside a burn or loch, where the kids were free to run and play. When choosing a site we learned that it was wise to examine the area chosen, not directly beneath a tree, nor too close to a burn or loch, but rather on open ground which was raised up. That way, should it rain heavily during the night we wouldn't get flooded out. We had seen that happen to campers many times. We had even seen some tents flattened by falling branches.

*Expendable*

Arriving at a camping exhibition is always an extraordinary sight. There in front of you, in a huge field, are row after row of very colourful tents, some small, others very large; many designed to resemble cottages, giving the feeling that you can have a second home in the country. The kids would always run on ahead of us calling to us to buy this one or that one, which we would have loved to.

Going around the exhibition, we talked as if we could have the tent of our choice, but we were soon brought back to earth with a bump when we looked at the price tab. The money thing got worse at the tea stall, where it cost me twelve shillings for two cups of cold tea and two small bottles of juice. We enjoyed the exhibition but decided we would have to save a bit longer should we wish to buy the tent we liked, and our grand tour of Europe would also have to wait a bit longer.

Back at work on Monday, I spent most of the day preparing the safety magazine. I had managed to collate enough articles and drawings to produce the first *Safety What?* I still hadn't got a name for it and I knew that I would have a lot of difficulties getting it produced or even getting the specifications printed. I had hoped to get help from Area Headquarters but I didn't think Smiley would agree. I couldn't expect assistance from the pit staff. We did have a clerk but to expect her to type out thirty pages of prose and six pages of illustrations, and then put them through a copier to produce a thousand magazines, was too much.

I decided I would have to go to Area and talk to the head of the typing pool, and then to the Area Safety Engineer, to accept his promise of help. You would not be blamed for wondering why I was taking all this hassle. First, I am told to do something, and then it's made virtually impossible for me to comply. I asked myself whether or not I should take the easy way out, and go direct to Area, in defiance of Smiley's wishes.

I could see little alternative except, perhaps, to go to Area and get just one copy produced. From that, I could then do the rest at the pit on our copier, but that would take ages with Smiley breathing down my neck. Anyway I hadn't the time and knew of nobody else who would do it. Thirty eight thousand pages in total; I know this should all have been thought out before it was decided to produce a magazine, but obviously this was not taken into account. I went home, still debating the solution.

Back at night school, the teacher seemed especially pleased to see us. I think she thought we had given it up. Actually, I would have liked to but I hadn't got the guts. At home, Ruth wasn't saying much. She was trying to give up smoking and she hadn't had a cigarette for two weeks. Usually when she said she would something she did it. There was little wonder that I could never get the better of her without drastic measures, causing her to go in a huff.

Next morning, at work, we received a visit from the Royal Navy, a Lieutenant and six Petty Officers. We had expected them at 9.30 am but it was 10.30 am before they arrived, all very smartly dressed in uniform, ready to go underground. They were a good lot, a bit formal to begin with but we soon made friends. They were from a Polaris submarine, Britain's nuclear deterrent, and when at sea they were on active service, patrolling the seas of the world. They were ready to strike, should they receive such orders.

I did not know till then that we had ships virtually at war readiness all the time. Their tour of duty on board was ten weeks at a spell, eight weeks continually underwater, whilst their route and destination remained a secret. Eddie came with me on the visit underground and was greatly interested in the eight weeks under water, away from female company.

"One gets used to it," said the young Lieutenant. "One certainly misses the female company, but really, it's all in the mind you know."

Eddie confessed that it would be far too much for him, to have to stay controlled for any length of time.

"Eight weeks would be like a life time to me," he admitted.

"It has its compensations," claimed the Lieutenant. "Although marriage is lived in only short spells at a time, it keeps the love warm and very much alive."

Eddie was not convinced.

"You navy types have the reputation of having a girl in every port. At least it's always there for me, even although I don't always get it."

They laughed and assured him that there were no ports for a submarine. The visit lasted for about four hours and they were a very tired bunch when they got back to the surface, and also a bit relieved. There was one incident during the visit that we thought was amusing, but they didn't think so.

It happened as we were walking along a roadway with a lot of water underfoot. It was running down the walls and we had to wade through it, the water being no higher that the top of our boots. For submariners to be underground, surrounded by water, was bad enough, but for the water to be rushing from the roof in sheets really upset them.

While showering in the pit head baths, I felt a tap on my shoulder. This was normal procedure. The person in the next cubicle would be trying to get attention, to get his back washed, and he would then wash yours. I was hesitating for a moment before turning round when a female voice shouted at me,

"Come on. I need your assistance. I have a man in here with a broken leg."

I spun round and standing in front of me was the colliery nurse.

"Come on," she urged. "Just wrap a towel around you."

I did as she said and followed her into the ambulance room. A man was on a stretcher on top of the table, his trousers and boots were off, his leg was badly out of line and he was groaning.

"I want you to hold him down while I give him a shot of morphine," she said, indicating his shoulder.

The injured man was protesting. He didn't want morphine.

"It will take the pain away and you will feel a lot better."

After she gave the injection she waited until it took effect then said, "The ambulance is on its way and in a moment I will try and straighten his leg, so hold him down."

After the injured man had been taken off to hospital and I was about to leave the ambulance room, she said to me, "I hope I didn't embarrass you earlier."

"No," I lied, hiding my face as I left.

*Expendable*

She called after me, "If you've seen one you've seen them all."
How could she say that? A thousand men use the showers, and
even I note the difference. I just kept walking to hide my
embarrassment, and recalled a time when, during the war, whilst
stationed at Cesentaca, our crew was given an operational flight to
Rome. Our task was to ferry a top brass army type and his secretary
to attend a conference, we were told. We liked the idea. It would be
a safe journey, with no flak to dodge, nor enemy fights on our tail,
and anyway I had never been to Rome, so it sounded good.

At the airfield, air pilot Jimbo Guthrie was in his cockpit doing
his checklist and getting the engines heated up. The navigator, Dave
Thomson, was in the nose checking out the route. The wireless
operator and I were standing outside the aircraft awaiting the arrival
of our passengers. When the staff car did appear, out stepped our
Commanding Officer followed by this gorgeous piece of crumpet,
(wow, was she nice) and then the top brass man. The car driver
opened the boot of the car and removed an overnight bag, two
parachutes and their harness. Our C.O. came forward and instructed
us to see that the harness was fitted and worn by all passengers.

"Yes Sir!"

We both spoke at the same time, trying to keep an eye on the
secretary. After a few more words with our guests, our C.O. shook
their hands, moved back into the staff car and drove off, leaving a
rather arrogant officer and a seemingly frightened secretary to our
mercy. He came forward, reluctantly, and shook hands with us,
rather more a slight touch than a firm grasp. It made us feel dirty.

"Look here, soldier," he said, "I should rather advise you that I
have never worn one of these things, a parachute I believe it is. Is it
absolutely necessary?"

We looked towards the pilot who seemed to be taking a keen
interest in the proceedings, with his head sticking out of the cockpit,
looking over his shoulder. He didn't speak, just nodded. Which was
a yes, they had got to be worn. Our top man, who was also looking
at our pilot, got the message.

"Well, damn it, if they have to be worn, get on with it," he
barked.

*Expendable*

The wireless operator and I were already kitted up for the flight, flying suit, boots and helmets with oxygen mask and parachute harness. The wireless operator put a harness on to the officer. It was fitted by putting two straps over the shoulders and rests midway down the body, with a third strap pulled up tightly between the legs; then all glitches connect into a release just about midway.

Now our aircraft was not fitted out to ferry passengers, and we had never done so in the past. So our guest would enter the aircraft via a hatch at the back under the tail and would have to sit on the floor.

Whilst the wireless operator was ushering the top brass into the aircraft, it dawned on me that I would have to fit the parachute harness onto the girl. I noticed that our pilot was still looking at us and the navigator had left his position in the nose to stand in front of the aircraft, both looking straight at me.

They looked a bit amused as though they were expecting something funny to happen, and to my embarrassment, and also to the girl's, it did. You see, she was wearing a skirt and I had to put my hand between her legs, get hold of the strap, pull it tight and clip it into place. By the time I had her harness fitted, her skirt was up to her thighs exposing her legs and part of her knickers. As she crawled into the aircraft she was doing her best to pull her skirt down, at least to try and hide her underwear.

Not a word was spoken about this predicament until we landed in Rome airport and our passengers had been picked up and hurried away. It was then that the ragging started.

Another adventure I recall from my time in Italy. There was a very important railway bridge in the north of the country, a bridge about a quarter of a mile across with a town situated at both ends, something like North and South Queensferry in Scotland. The bridge was of the utmost importance to the Germans as it was their escape route to the north. They realised that should the bridge be destroyed they would have to stand and fight or surrender as the British forces were closing fast.

Our Squadron was given the task of taking it out, a simple job we thought, with six aircraft. It had been agreed at briefing that instead of bombing along the line of the bridge, which looked like a slim pencil from the air, we would fly at right angles to it, and in that way with all six aircraft dropping their bombs at the same time, some short, others over, the in betweens should land on the target.

Now a bridge, as important as our target was, had got to be protected and we expected to be challenged by German fighter aircraft as we approached the target and by anti aircraft fire over the target. We all knew what to expect and were pretty well tensed up. The planners of the raid had known the risks and had allowed us an escort of Spitfires, for which we were very grateful.

Flying in formation at thirteen thousand feet, escorted by our Spitfires, with not a cloud in the sky, just a pale blue roof over our heads, all crisp and clear, we were feeling secure that the Spitfires could take care of any attack by enemy aircraft. As we approached the target area, the Spitfires hung back and let us go on alone. We all knew that during our bombing run we would be quite safe from attack by enemy fighters but not from anti - aircraft fire.

From thirteen thousand feet, the squadron would dive down to ten thousand feet and level off for a bomb run of ten to twenty seconds, straight and level, in order to get an accurate aim on the target. When the leading bomb aimer has the target lined up, he will fire a Very pistol as the signal to the squadron to release their bombs. You may be wondering why only a few seconds to do a bomb run.

Well, it's because a flight has to fly straight and level to drop its bombs accurately, but whilst in this position planes are sitting ducks for anti-aircraft fire, which means that the shorter the bomb run, the safer. Now the Germans know this and wait until the bomb run starts. Then up comes the flak. They don't fire at the aircraft but ahead of them causing the aircraft to fly through their bombardment. That's the time when we put our heads down to avoid, if possible, the wall of shrapnel ahead. It's like running the gauntlet.

I was pretty well protected with armoured plating all around my turret and a German steel helmet on my head. The navigator bomb aimer wore a flak jacket under his overalls, which afforded him some protection but would be useless should the aircraft receive a direct hit and get shot down. We didn't receive a direct hit nor were we shot down and all the bombs were dropped on the lead bomb aimers signal. Then, it was a rush to get back to the safety of our escort.

Landing back at our airfield, we made a check of the damage, then went off to debriefing with the intelligence people. We felt that we had hit the target but hadn't stayed around long enough to confirm. Two things were made plain to us after the raid. One, the spitfires had engaged German fighters and had come off best, but one spitfire had been damaged. Fortunately, he made it back to base. The second piece of news, confirmed by aerial photos, was that we had not damaged the bridge. We'd missed, which meant that we had to go back and do it again.

This time we were sure that we had knocked it out. However, again the reconnoitre photos showed that the bridge was still serviceable. Now this was a bit embarrassing, and our reputation at stake, so to even things up we had a third go at it. To our sheer embarrassment, we were told that the bridge was again, still serviceable. We could only think that the Germans were repairing the damage as fast as we were creating it.

To bring this story to a head, the war in Italy was over and our squadron had to move north. The pilots flew our aircraft to the new site taking with them all our gear, the remainder of us, including the ground crew, travelled north by train and were somewhat surprised to learn that we would cross the river over the bridge we tried so hard to knock out, the same bridge that nearly took away our reputation.

This we wanted to see, so approaching the bridge we were all crowding the windows, eager to see this defiant object, and fearful that it would take its revenge on us and collapse into the river. But no, it still stood, proud and erect, and allowed us to pass over its whole length. It hadn't got off scot-free, the side railings had been blown away and only one track was in use. The train passed over slowly as though in a mark of respect. And the towns that stood at either end of the bridge? Well they were both gone, not a single house or a tree left standing, all having been obliterated by our bombs. Only large craters remained. In wartime, it is not a good idea to live in a town which is close to an important bridge.

The next day started with a bang. Two men were injured before it was daylight. One had a crushed hand, the other had rolled on a belt conveyor whilst illegally riding it. This could easily happen when someone decided to do this instead of walking, as there was not always the clearance between the conveyor and the roof to allow a man to pass between. In this instance, we feared for the man's back and so we very quickly got him attended to in the ambulance room and sent both injured men off to hospital.

We discussed their injuries as the ambulance drove off and decided that the man with the injured hand would be all right, no bones broken. The other would be kept in the hospital, and that gave rise to another problem. His wife and family would not be aware that he was injured until one of us went round to tell them and, you guessed it, I was the one told to go. I didn't enjoy these visits, knocking on a door just before daylight, with only bad news to report.

The worst part was when the door was first opened to me and I introduced myself. The wife would always start to panic before I could tell her what had happened. I would quickly advise her that there was no need to panic; that he had only hurt his back, which was true, but also untrue. The kids would be sent off to school and I would drive her to the hospital where I would wait until she was ready to go home.

Back at the colliery, I had to go to see Smiley again. He had been pushing the magazine but he wouldn't allow me to go to the typing pool. His motto was, don't put the colliery in the limelight when things are not doing so well.

"Keep a low profile," he maintained.

Anyway I finally got him to agree. He had too much on his mind, too much to think about that was of far more importance than whether allowing me to go to Area would make matters any worse.

At Area, I met the typing pool supervisor, whom I had telephoned earlier. We discussed the layout of the magazine and she introduced me to the girl who would do the work, advising me to give her a few days. Back at the pit I was feeling a bit pleased with myself. In spite of all the hassle it had not robbed me of a sense of achievement.

Eddie and Frank were in the office when I got back, having a quiet moment with no immediate pressure on them. I joined their conversation, which was steered by Eddie onto his favourite subject, sex and dating. He attended the local Miners Welfare regularly, a first class club, run entirely by a very successful committee, which, as a matter of fact, was the same committee who run the N.U.M.

There were many attractions laid on in the club for the miners and their wives: indoor bowling, concerts, film shows, which you remember we took part in, dancing and of course, booze at much below the normal price. Although there were many differences at the pit between the miners' union and management, they were never shown nor discussed in the club. Should any member of the pit management show themselves at the club they were treated like V.I.Ps. This committee, it seemed to me, had a firm hold of the men both at the pit and during their leisure time. They had it all sewn up.

Another attraction, well you could call it that, was the Sunday night dance night. *Grab a Granny* some wit called it, and the name stuck. That was Eddie's favourite night, and it became so popular that, it was rumoured, busloads of 'girls' would travel miles just to be at the dance. That's what Eddie told us, but knowing him we had to take everything he said with a pinch of salt. He was not a liar exactly, just exaggerated a wee bit. Another thing he told us was that each week a raffle was run in the club, with the first prize being a week on the committee.

We discussed many topics apart from Eddie's pet subjects, including the solar system, how the earth, travelling at over six thousand miles per hour through space could meet up with a comet coming from the opposite direction. We discussed how this would bring an end to all the problems of mankind - including Eddie's sexual desires.

"But what of God, wouldn't He stop this comet thing from hitting us?"

"We would hope so," both Frank and I said at the same time.

*Expendable*

Eddie was staggered.

"I have never thought of anything like that before. It would frighten me to let my mind dwell on the world coming to an end," he said, aghast.

I received a draft copy of the magazine. I had called it *A Design for Safety*. Smiley accepted it in full, with only one exception which I would have to remove and replace with another item. He insisted that I keep it still to thirty pages, including the illustrations.

I was now forced to find others from outside the colliery to contribute. This thing could go on for ever and I couldn't afford to spend much more time on it. I sent letters to the Safety Branch at Area, to the Head of Mines Rescue, and to the big chief in London. They couldn't refuse, could they?

My son Raymond, who had been at art college and worked at the colliery office, had assisted me in preparing the stencil drawings and I got him to prepare some more whilst I awaited replies from my letters asking for help. Within a week I had everything tied up and off to the typing pool again. In two more days the magazine had been printed and was ready for me to collect in huge bundles of loose leaves. All that remained now was to get the loose sheets made up into book form and issued. That, of course, was providing Smiley agreed. I was getting a bit sick now.

Smiley must not try to make any more alterations, or I would just give up. I was not running back to the typing pool again, no way. That was it as far as I was concerned. I made up just two copies and took them to Smiley. He liked it, so I got the office staff together to have the loose sheets made up into books and distributed.

What was written in the magazine had already annoyed some people at the colliery. They had popped in to the office for a preview and didn't like what was written about them and their department.

"Good," I thought, "I didn't aim to please."

The magazine had been intended to promote safety, and to provoke people into thinking more about their safety standards. This was not always popular, but it had to be done, no matter who got in the way. I really didn't know what they were troubled about. I had thought this issue was mild and amusing. They said it would cause disharmony and could only add to the troubles at the colliery.

"Just wait until we get going with the next issue," advised Smiley.

"What next issue?" I said, "No. Please no more!"

"It's worth all the hassle," said Smiley. "Look how we have got them all going. The next issue will aim to annoy a lot more people."

I imagined the Unions doing their nut about this first publication, but I was proved wrong. The N.U.M. were quite happy about it and we were getting the not-so-good feed back from the tradesmen. Eddie and Frank disassociated themselves from anything to do with the magazine because of the criticism.

"I hope the production of the magazine did not interfere with your duties," the production manager commented

Within a week a Mines Inspector arrived at the pit and I spent most of the day with him. He left happy, with a copy of the magazine, and said that he would wish to contribute to the next issue. I thought that he had come to check me out.

With the magazine off my hands, and no intention of starting a second one right away, I now had time to get on with other work. From the colliery to the main line, a rail track was laid to allow a train and wagons to enter the colliery confines. The line was about two miles long and required to be inspected regularly. It was not British Rail's responsibility to inspect or repair the track. That belonged to us.

Smiley insisted that inspections be made regularly, as an incident a few years back had caused the death of a child. The track ran alongside the village and often children were tempted over it, into the field beyond. It was protected by a high netted fence that had been, from time to time, damaged and repaired.

It was this track that Eddie and I were about to inspect when we saw the chief engineer and the surface foreman hurrying to Smiley's office. Something was up, and it wasn't long before we found out what it was. The explosive magazine had been broken into and explosives taken. The magazine is situated some two hundred yards from the colliery. It sits in a depression and is built like a fortress, surrounded by a high metal fence, with the uprights fitted close together. It looked impregnable and everyone thought that it was, but it had somehow been broken into.

This was a serious matter, and once again, anybody who was somebody was called to the pit, including the Chiefs from Area, police, C.I.D. and some other gentlemen in black who nobody knew anything about. Fortunately, no detonators were taken even though they were housed in the same building. The police started their investigation by questioning everyone who was associated with the explosive store. We could not believe that anyone at the colliery would steal explosives. The officials handle them every day and if they wanted explosives it was a simple matter of helping themselves. Sure, there was a system for checking the amount of explosives used, but that could easily be overcome. The officials had too much respect for explosives to dabble in them.

Whatever the police found out, we were not to know. It was bandied about that the explosives were taken by the I.R.A, but surely they didn't need to go to such lengths to obtain them? They would have their own means of supply. We found out how the intruders got into the magazine but heard no more of the break in until the police came to the colliery in a police van and informed us that they had found the explosives.

In the back of their van they showed us a ten gallon oil drum crammed with the stolen explosives, which were weeping and in dangerous state. The police asked us to remove them as they were not familiar with explosives. With Eddie's reluctant assistance, I took the drum to a place three hundred yards from the colliery with the police and Smiley following behind. We set the explosives down in a depression which had been caused by previous explosions. Getting rid of old and weeping explosives was routine to us. I fetched six ounces of explosives and a detonator, which I made positive and put into the drum. Then, using two hundred yards of cable and posting four sentries to secure the area, I turned the key in the battery. There was a flash, a roar, a cloud of smoke and dirt falling to the ground. It was over. Smiley returned to his office.

"Just another bloody day in the life of Camdon," he said.

The police never told us how they came by the explosives. We could only surmise that they had a tip-off. We were never told who the men in black were. We suspected that they were M.I.5 or M.I.6. Imagine, top secret men coming to our pit that we should cause such an upset to the nation. This should have put us on the map, but nothing was ever reported in the newspapers, and in a short while it was all forgotten.

Smiley was having a difficult time of late. We could see that he was under a lot of pressure from the goings on at the pit. No one could blame him, it had been hard going, and little wonder that he didn't flip his lid. He became aggressive, and swore more that usual, with the staff taking the brunt of his wrath. He reminded me of a previous boss I had, well, not exactly a boss, more of an R.A.F. corporal.Before we went on leave, the sten gun was part of our training and there was an adopted procedure at the range for firing. We had a very fierce looking corporal to take us through the stages and his language was also fierce. We were lined up on the range, facing the target, with the corporal to the rear of us, bawling.

"Now, listen to me, you bastards. On this range you will do exactly what I tell you to do, because I don't want to be shot by one of you pricks. Is that clear?"

The sten gun was on the ground at our feet and we were then given a full magazine.

"First, pick up your sten gun, fingers off the trigger. Now clip in the magazine and do not fire until I give the word. Is everybody clear on that? Now, the important part, with the gun in your hand you will never point it anywhere except at the target. While you are firing, should the gun jam, stand perfectly still and hold up your right arm. Do not turn round to face me and tell me your gun has jammed. If you do I will shove it so far up your arse you'll be shitting bullets for a week."

# CHAPTER TWELVE
## NIGHTMARE

While I was still pondering over the strikes, I was informed that Smiley wanted to see me. In his office he told me that there was a man in the pithead baths getting ready to go underground, who was drunk. I looked at Smiley with a puzzled frown.

"Go and stop him, get the police if you have to."

"Who is it?" I asked.

Smiley named him and I just stood there, unable to believe he was putting this problem on to me.

"Will you need help?"

I remained silent, still trying to take this on board.

"Well, will you?" urged Smiley.

No, I don't want an audience to watch me being thumped, I thought.

"No, I shall do it quietly or otherwise he might think we'll gang up on him and turn nasty."

As I approached the pit head baths the backshift men, knowing what was going on, were watching in keen anticipation. They seemed to me to be wondering whether to alert the first aid room or call in an ambulance for me. As I walked up the dirty side, where the pit clothes lockers were, the men dressing to go down the pit were indicating to me by signalling and pointing to where the drunk was. I spotted him standing in the middle of the aisle, sort of doubled up with his shirt pulled over his head.

Walking up to him I helped him with his shirt, his head popped out and he turned a glazed stare on me. He was truly drunk. He didn't speak, he couldn't.

"Come on, let's go home," I said.

He was too drunk to argue and too drunk to be aggressive for which I was ever grateful. I helped him to undress from his pit gear, and assisted him back to the clean lockers where I got him to dress and then left him sitting while I went to the union office, to get someone to take him home. What a time it took me to convince them that it was as much their problem as management's, and sticking in a wee bit about the police for good measure. Finally they agreed, just in time as well, because we found our man back in the dirty side with his pit clothes on again. They drove him home, pit clothes and all.

Thankfully, incidents of this nature are not common as miners, in general, take underground work seriously, something for which I, in particular, am eternally grateful. But it has to be said that miners do indulge in a dram or two, especially at the weekends. Saturday night is *the* night in the Miners welfare for drinking and dancing, drinking and singing and just drinking. It was what they did, it helped to clear their throats of all the dust swallowed during the week. Sunday was the other main Welfare night, when the evening was passed listening and watching the well organised entertainment that was put on for their enjoyment.

Discipline is at a premium during the weekend period in the Miners' Welfare. Well, maybe discipline is too strong a word. I should have said the committee kept an eye open for any disruption. It had happened in the past where an argument had led to an all out battle. Anyone getting out of hand was speedily rejected and later called up in front of the committee to be given a warning. The committee handled its own problems.

Back at work on Monday morning, the first hour was spent going over the happenings of the weekend when enormous amounts of alcohol had been drunk. Well, listening to them, you would have been inclined to think so. But again, I have known some who could put away twelve pints at a sitting. My tipple is a wee goldie, as it is known, the spirit of life. But even whisky has got to be restricted as it has a sting in its tail.

Restrictions were all forgotten about at that special time of the year, Auld Year's Night. Christmas was also celebrated, but in a much nicer and quieter way, and you didn't have to stay up all night. New Year, 'After the bells' as it was known, was when your home became an open house to everyone and anyone who wished to call. Nobody was ever turned away.

*Expendable*

Our home was always full at the New Year where the neighbours would congregate. At times, it felt like there were thousands of them. When someone called at your door after twelve, the custom was for the visitor to bring a bottle with him. Some say only a dark headed person or somebody with a piece of coal would be welcomed, but don't you believe it. When a person entered your home, he would give the man of the house a dram out his bottle. Can you imagine taking a half from that many people? You don't of course. What I did was to put their half aside until later, when it would replenish the Punch Bowl. On such occasions it was filled with a punch made up of a bottle of whisky, two bottles of cider, four bottles of lemonade, ice and fruit.

It made an excellent punch and nobody got drunk too quickly when drinking from it, making for a very pleasant evening. Another advantage was that you didn't have to keep filling glasses all night, and people just helped themselves. Obviously the bowl might have to be refilled from time to time and you kept your eye on it, as one of your guests might think it a bit weak and pour an extra half bottle into it. Then you'd have a house full of drunk people.

Now take my advice and never hold a New Year party in your own house. Hold it in someone else's house, because after all the bodies have left at daybreak, you are left with a whole lot of cleaning up to do and, of course, a hangover.

New Year wouldn't be the same without a clootie dumpling. As far back as I can remember, there was always a clootie dumpling at the New Year, and only at the New Year. What was not eaten at the time would be sliced up and fried for breakfast.

Weekend drinking did little to make things seem any better at Camdon. Plans for the new development, which was the hope for the future, turned out to be faulty. They would be uneconomical in the production of coal. A new face was started up but only lasted for a month before it struck a major fault. Further drivages were started but they too came up against the same brick wall. The situation became hopeless, with nowhere to turn, resulting in pit meetings with all the unions.

There were question to be answered. Surely, it was argued, the board should have known of these faults in the area. The Board did know but insisted that the fault must have taken a huge swing and turned into the workings at Camdon. It looked like the end.

Everyone knew that the pit would close, that it was just a matter of time. The coal which we mined was getting too far away from the pit bottom, adding to the problem that there were too many faults in the strata. The Coal Board laid down the policy that where a coal face could not be worked for at least four hours in any shift, it would require to be stopped as it would not be viable.

That meant that the time the workmen took to travel from the pit-head to the coal face and the time it took the men at the end of the shift to travel to the surface, taken off the total time available underground, must leave at least four hours in which to work at the coal face. Otherwise, close down was inevitable.

It was not all go during those long work days, as I sometimes tend to make out. No, there were times when we could relax and work at a slower pace, instead of flying around trying to do two or three things at once and only priorities could be tackled. Then again, managers in general were inclined to make everything for you a priority. Anyway it was on one of those relaxing days, when I was updating records and quite happy to be left alone, when work was found for my idle hands.

At this time, I was at a surface mine that was still under development, that is, the roads were still being driven and not yet into production. I was aware that the manager, under manager, chief engineer and a salesman were all in the manager's office having a coffee and I was asked to join them. When I got there they were having a noisy discussion. The manager was on his feet with a golf club in his hand and as I walked in, they walked out. The under manager told me to stay in the office to stand by the phone, and then he was off as well.

I watched them make their way to the field that was just behind the offices, still arguing. I was to learn later that the salesman was a pretty good golfer, a three handicap I'm told. The Manager and company were all good golfers but in no way as good as the salesman. Apparently the argument, discussion if you like, was how far an amateur could hit a golf ball with a seven iron and not stray from the line. Whilst I was sitting there, deep in thought, amazed at how relaxed we were that day, I was aware of a knock at the door. As I sat up, a figure came in to the office, a well dressed man with a brief case. He walked towards me with his hand outstretched.

"Good morning, Mister Manager. I am Smith, the new Mines Inspector."

I was caught off balance, and totally lost for a response. He took his hat off, and I gestured with my hand for him to take a seat. He looked at me curiously, and I found my voice. "I am not the Colliery Manager. He is out in the yard and I am only here to stand by the phone. I will go and find him and let him know that you are here."

Before I went, I put the kettle on to make coffee, then nipped behind the office and did the hundred yards in two seconds flat. I told them of the visitor and they scattered. I returned to the Manager's office and informed the Inspector that the Manager was on his way. I prepared a pot of coffee and left.

There was always a near panic when a Mines Inspector dropped in for a visit. He was supposed to give notice of his coming plus an indication of what he intended to look at. There was also an Electrical Inspector and a Mechanical Inspector of Mines who visited frequently and we could be well prepared for them, given notice. At the end of the day, the man responsible for the day to day running of the pit was the Colliery Manager, and a Mines Inspector could cause a lot of problems for a manager when he submitted his report to his boss. I suppose that was why we treated them with the greatest respect, the swines. But, to be honest, most inspectors were very understanding, as they themselves, at least most of them, had been Colliery Managers at one time.

Sometimes, at this same mine, on a Friday afternoon after a long frustrating week, a wee dram would not go amiss for the managers. But not for me, I had to hang back and drive them home.

Other days, the manager would look into my office and say, "Get your pit clothes on, we're going underground."

If I were to start to protest, he would not have any of it.

"Just meet me at the top of the mine in five minutes. Be there!"

*Expendable*

I would change and be ready at the top of the mine, within the five minutes, but he was always already there, with the empty mine cars waiting.

"Jump in."

We were lowered down the mine. We didn't have a man-riding system at that time so what we were doing was illegal, but he was the boss. Walking inby, we came to a coal drivage that had not been long started. It had been driven to fifteen feet from the main roadway, and no conveyor had yet been installed so the coal had to be cast out twice to the main belt before loading.

"Right, this is as far we go for the next hour, grab a shovel, let's see if the office work has softened you up. This will test you."

I said nothing, but determined to show that I was still fit enough to do a hard day's work. It was killing me but we kept it up and after an hour we had it all shovelled out to the belt. It would take another hour to get the coal cleared up and filled away and I was finding out that determination does not eliminate tiredness.

Fortunately, the manager got to his feet.

"Come on, we'll go. We have other drivages to visit."

We visited a further three headings but this time didn't get involved with the physical side of the job, for which I was grateful. I didn't tell you the name of the manager or under manager and I don't intend to, but I can tell you they were great men, well-respected by their workmen and their peers.

I suppose you are wondering about the golf argument. Well, I can tell you that it was the salesman who won. One hundred and fifty yards, and only six feet off line.

All that I have written about happened at least twenty five years ago, but I never forget. My favourite nightmare, which, I suppose, is common to all miners is to be buried alive underground in a pit fall, where with the roof slowly coming down on top of you. You are trapped, you try to escape, but there is no way out. You crawl here, then over there, but to no avail, and with the solid roof coming down ever so much closer, you feel it crushing, crushing, and then you wake up and in a cold sweat, discover gratefully that the duvet is lying heavily on top of you. I don't think the nightmares will ever go away; they'll probably be with me for the rest of my life.

What a way of life - and in my day it was for life. When you joined the pit as a young man, that was you until you retired. It was a very dangerous occupation, life threatening at times, where if an inexperienced miner was careless he would certainly get clobbered. In the past, I have helped to stretcher out injured miners and sometimes dead miners, and in the latter case you are so overcome that you want to get away as far as possible from the pit and never look back. It takes days to get over that awful feeling, but in the end you always go back. In my case I had a far better life during my interlude in the R.A.F. but I still went back.

So are miners born and bred into the mines without the opportunity of some other life? It would seem that way and yet, some have left the mines, found other work and never looked back. They cannot be blamed for leaving. I have seen strippers hewing out coal from a two and a half foot seam, lying on their side, swinging a pick and with water dropping on them from the roof, sweating in heavy oil skins, neck and wrists scadded from the rubbing of the oil skins, for eight long hours a day. Very few did leave, but one at least gave it up and emigrated to Canada.

I can recall one incident when a man died before we got him to the surface. Hearing a call for help from the coal face where there had been a fall, we raced up the face line to where it was and found a man was buried beneath it. While we clawed at the rubble to release him, two others were trying to steady the roof which was still falling, until we managed to haul him clear and drag him down the face to safety.

I have witnessed a colliery manager and an oversman grappling on the waste side of the face conveyor, swapping punches and curses, helmets trailing with the lamps still attached as they rolled between the packs, unaware of the danger they put themselves in, and all because the oversman stopped the conveyor, and coal production, to do a slight repair. The Manager, who was on the face at the time, was furious because he couldn't get an answer to why the conveyor had stopped, and when he found out that the oversman was to blame an argument started. That gives you an idea of the pressure a colliery manager was under each day, to make the production target. I should tell you that those two were the best of friends, normally.

I have also witnessed an engineering feat which I thought would not be possible. A coal face, two hundred yards long, and four feet high ran into a fault, a two foot upthrow. The fault cut across the face at an angle and was only exposed a few feet at a time. The face then was two feet of stone and two feet of coal and had to be carried over the whole of the two hundred yards, with the edge of the fault on the roof and very unstable. It could have dropped in without warning. And those were the good old days they tell us, before mechanisation, before discos, powered sports, shearers and drill rigs, just sweat and slog.

The coal had to be taken out, a bit at a time, to get enough room for the armoured face conveyor, the powered supports and the shearer to be lifted up on to the new floor and all the time keeping a close watch on the roof. Impossible I thought, but it was done; and the face was back to normal and nobody was injured in the process. Beautiful.

Supporting the roof underground is not always easy, and sometimes impossible. For example, a coal face has to keep advancing rapidly. With the coal extracted and the powered supports advanced the roof will break up and collapse up to the line of the powered supports which will be held temporarily. The face advances on a broad two hundred yard front leaving a very large area behind unsupported. It can't be held up and collapses.

As the roof fractures and breaks up behind the coal face, the fractures or breaks extend in advance of it. It is therefore important that the face keeps advancing. When a face stops for any length of time, say, holidays, strikes, or whatever, the waste will catch up putting a lot of stress on the supports and the face will break in advance of the face-line. Holidays over, it takes a few days of cautious advance before the face is back to normal.

It is not only at the coal face where the roof causes problems. In roadways which are supported by circle arch girders, where the floor is soft, the pressure from the roof will cause the girders to gradually sink into the floor, causing the floor, or pavement, to heave up, buckling the rail track and standing equipment. The floor has to be dug up and tracks re-laid without interrupting production.

Little wonder I have nightmares of being buried alive underground, and you will understand more when I tell you of this next true episode. At a pit where I worked, one three foot high section had been worked out and abandoned but it was still being ventilated and was supported by timber straps and trees and, when last visited, it was stable. However, the Colliery Manager sent the Ventilation Officer down to this face to check it out, to see if it was still stable and ventilated.

Half an hour later, the Manager, having second thoughts about sending a man to the abandoned area on his own, told me to go down and accompany the Officer into this no mans land. He had a half hour start on me, so I had to hurry to catch up with him and as I arrived at the bottom of the main gate I was out of breath and sat down to rest.

There was no sign of him. I looked up the face-line. Nothing. No light reflection. He must be well ahead of me and already half way up. I wasn't sure what to do. He couldn't be that far ahead of me, I was thinking, unless something had happened to him. He could be buried up there so I decided I had better go up the face-line as he might need my help. Putting those stupid thoughts out my mind I got down and started to crawl up the face-line.

It was three feet high in places, but it seemed a lot lower in others. My back kept touching the roof, reducing me almost to a belly crawl, and the whole place was dark, silent, eerie, and empty. It always feels, in this situation, like you are the only person there. I couldn't see very far ahead as my head was down and I couldn't look up due to the roof height, so I could only see a few feet in front of me.

I had my flame lamp with me, of course, which was looking very healthy with no sign of carbon monoxide gas. The air was passing up the face leading me to believe that the run was still open and I thought that if I came up against a fall I'd turn back, but I didn't. The first small fall of roof I came up against was where two sets of wood had collapsed at the waste and spilled onto the face.

I hesitated for a moment then crawled around it to safer ground. I continued to crawl on, knowing that I was about half way up and I didn't like the look of the trees - many on the waste side were broken and others at an angle with the roof, down to about two and a half feet. Being careful not to touch anything lest I should cause a fall, I continued, calling myself all the idiots for even attempting this and cursing the V.O.

I stopped for a moment, lying on my stomach to get my breath back. I felt as if I were trapped in a dog's kennel, as my movements were very restricted. My flame lamp was still looking healthy and that was the only thing going for me. As I lay there, it was weird, and very, very quiet. I decided I had better keep going, it's better than lying and letting your mind dwell on morbid thoughts.

I began crawling again, my knees and hands taking a bit of punishment. I should have been wearing kneepads but there is nothing like a wee bit of discomfort to keep your mind focused. Then I saw it - a huge fall of roof right in front of me. I stopped and stared at it. I was amazed how calm I felt, but I think I was too stunned to feel anything. I crawled forward to have a better look and noted that there were no large stones amongst the debris. It was all small stuff, which tends to spread out. I could see that it was not closed tight, that I could look up to the top of the fall and see the solid roof above it. The air was rushing through, although there was no way around the fall. The only way was over the top. I could tell that it was not a recent fall, well - maybe only a few days old, because it had settled. I looked up into the cavity and shone my light to the other end which allowed me to estimate the length of it. I took it to be ten to twelve feet. I backed out and wondered what I should do.

All thoughts of the V.O. were out of my mind. I was too preoccupied with my own situation. I knew that I was near the top road which could be as near as forty yards away, and it was a hundred and fifty yards to the Main Gate, back the way I had come. I had another look at the fall and decided to go over it. I know what you are thinking, that I was off my rocker; and I would now agree with you, but remember you do things sometimes that you don't want to do. And that is where my nightmare comes in.

I got to the top all right and started to slide down the other side on my stomach - and got stuck. My helmet fell off and as I stretched out to retrieve it my shoulder bumped against an unstable support which dropped out, bringing down debris on to my back. I lay still, afraid to move lest I bring down more. Fortunately it was all small stuff and gave me a better opening to escape, which I did, dragging my helmet with me. I reached the tail gate in jig time and lay down to rest and said a silent prayer.

The irony here is that the ventilation officer didn't go in the main gate and up the run. Oh, no, he went in the tail gate to the top road, went down the run, saw the fall, turned back and went off to report. After my harrowing experience, I just kept quiet about and didn't tell anyone. I would only have got criticism and certainly no sympathy.

# CHAPTER THIRTEEN
## PLAYTIME

Perhaps you are thinking that I have made it look like all work and no play, but it was not like that, we did get time off and we took full advantage of it. Our main pastime was fishing from a boat in a loch, and if you must fish what better place than in Scotland with its four thousand lochs. It is estimated that there are more fishermen in Scotland that there are football supporters. Of course there are other activities in Scotland apart from fishing. There's golf. But fishing is prohibited from September to March and you can't very well play golf in the snow, so what the hell are you supposed to do between September and March?

A friend once said to me that fishing was the most peaceful activity on the planet. He would say that, sitting beside a loch on a warm summer's evening when the sun is thinking that it's time to sink beyond the hills, when silence is contentment which fills your soul, and if you catch a fish that is a bonus. You are probably aware that there are many types of fishing and many types of fishermen. Basically, there are four types, or ways, of fishing. There's fly fishing, practised by the true angler, you'll always recognise him, with his hat full of flies. Then there is the lure, the artificial minnow, very useful with the spinning reel; a type of fishing banned on many lochs. Eddie used the under-stone fly, the common garden worm, which was always banned. There are another two methods of fishing that I know of. I'll tell you about them later.

Here is something I think is puzzling about fish: are they colour blind? Experts believe that they fish are not but I imagine that a fish, looking up to the surface of the water, would see a fly against the bright background of the sky as black, so why all the colours? Eddie's favourite bait, the under-stone fly is very successful, he maintains that all the big fish are hungry and want a feed of a big juicy worm not a tiny morsel of a fly. He never went home empty handed.

I went fishing in my spare time, usually with Eddie or Smiley, who away from the pit is quite normal, almost like a human being. Fishing lets him unwind. Eddie just loves fishing; I believe it's the love of his life. We would arrange to meet on a Saturday and set off to Aberfoyle where there are a couple of great lochs, and we would fish the whole day. Long before we would reach the loch, Eddie would have his rod built, eager to get on the water, or rather the bank; he was at home fishing from there. Smiley and I would take to the boat and it didn't matter if it rained or not. We would cast away in great anticipation. We would usually get a catch with small fish being thrown back into the loch, but sometimes we would go home empty handed. Of course there is always the chance that your wife begins to wonder if it was fish you were after. Women don't understand about these things.

Smiley was strictly a purist and only fished the fly. He could cast his line dropping his fly exactly where he wanted it. He was good. There was one other man whom I fished with who could better him at casting a fly, and he was the all Ireland champion. When he was fishing I could only watch and admire. He also was a nice guy.

Most lochs in Scotland have fish in abundance, but require a day's motoring to get there, and an overnight stay providing you had the time, and obviously we didn't. There is a fine loch that we used a lot, teeming with brown trout near Leslie in Fife. When you hired the loch it was yours for that day, the whole loch with the boat thrown in, all for six pounds. We took many a fish from that loch with Eddie very much in the lead when it came to capacity. He would only stop when it was too dark to see and even then Smiley and I had virtually to drag him away.

It was not always fair weather and sunny days, but more likely to be wet and blowy with the water being too rough to take the boat out. Once there was only a breeze when we started out, but, as evening was closing in, with us in the middle of the loch, the breeze turned into a hurricane, well, maybe not but blowing hard enough to put the wind up us. Worse still it was taking us further down the loch. The water was rough, really rough; we had been on rough water before but nothing like the waves we were getting then.

The boat was being tossed about and, unless we could get off the water soon, we didn't want to think about what might happen. We soon realised that it was hopeless to attempt to row against the wind, we just had to let it take us to the opposite shore. Thankfully, we grounded the boat and hauled it out of the water. Cold and wet and gathering up our gear we headed for the far end of the loch, which we knew would take us some time. Looking across the loch to where we had left Eddie, we could see nothing. Everything was shrouded in gloom as we set off for a very long walk, an hour and a half, to where we had left the car.

There are other times, out fishing on a loch, when there is no wind, not even a breeze, the water flat, reflecting the hills around you. No fish are rising. You get tired casting, and just sit and look at the water. If there are any fish in the loch, they are not where you are, and you are left wondering where can they have got to? And of course, your mind is thinking: couldn't science come up with something to make them feed? Or some portable contraption to allow you to catch them? After too many calm days on the water, I did come up with a couple of gadgets to assist in the catching of fish. The first was a multi-hook system with a different type of bait on each hook. I even put a piece of chopped pork from my sandwich on one hook, a piece of bread on another, and baited the remaining hooks with a variety of other tasty morsels, grubs and the under-stone fly. A single line from my rod was attached to the centre of two crossed wire coat hangers, and from each end of the coat hangers nylon was hung, with baited hooks all set at different depths.

The system had a twofold method of recording. What type of bait were the fish interested in, and what depth were they feeding at? But alas, I was never to record the findings of my experiment, for as I lowered the gear into the water my fly rod doubled and almost snapped, I was forced to act quickly and cut my line and it all sank to the bottom of the loch. I maintained that a huge fish took my bait, but Eddie and Smiley ridiculed the idea and said the whole contraption was far too heavy.

Before we set off on our next trip, Smiley told me that if I had any more gadgets to try out, and I was caught by the bailie, the police or the men in white coats, then I was on my own. You see I hadn't told him of my latest attempt, but I was certain he would approve once he saw it in action. It was a four inch square of plywood with a small hole in the middle. Into this hole I had stuck a wooden tooth pick with a small red flag on top. On the underside I hammered in a small staple to which I attached a three feet length of nylon with a baited hook on the end.

Now the principle is very simple. The plywood float is placed in the loch with the staple on top and the flag in the water, the nylon is wrapped once around the float and is then left to work for you. When a fish takes the bait, pulling on the nylon, the plywood float would right itself, and up would pop the red flag indicating a catch. Brilliant, eh?

Eddie was in the boat with me, and Smiley was on the bank. He was not getting involved. I had made six of these contraptions and Eddie helped to lay them in the water. If they worked he would put a dozen of them into action. I explained to him that this was only a bit of fun and, although it appeared that I was serious, it wasn't so.

Anyway, it would take the skill out of fishing. I knew that Eddie would not forsake the two rods he always took on a fishing trip. He loved the sport, hooking a trout was one thing, but bringing it in was something else. By this time all the floats were emigrating all over the loch and it was difficult to keep them within sight, so we just sat and waited.

Eddie shouted "Look, over there. There is a little red flag showing."

He was right, this could be our first catch, I thought. Picking up the oars and rowing towards the flag, I took a quick glance to the bank to give Smiley the thumbs up. I stopped half way with my arm half raised, telling Eddie to stop rowing and get the rods out. As I looked to where Smiley was, there were now two figures and Smiley was waving to us to come in. We recognised his companion. It was the water bailie.

"Do you think he has seen us?" I asked Eddie.

"No, we're too far away, anyway I hope he hasn't," he replied.

Taking the boat to the side and getting out, we were faced by a huge man with a weather beaten face, dressed in a shower coat with a gamekeeper's hat on his head.

"I have just been telling your partner here," he said, indicating Smiley, "that there are only two rods allowed on this loch at any one time, and you have three."

There were actually four counting Eddie's two. He seemed to be waiting for a reply, but we didn't give any. We just stood there with his eyes staring into us. It started to rain, it had rained off and on all day but we were too busy to notice it. The silence was awful; then Smiley got his hip flask out and offered the bailie a dram, which was readily accepted. That broke the ice and took the dourness from his face.

I was looking over my shoulder towards the loch, anxious about my traps; Eddie was feeling the same. The bailie was on his second dram and telling us that a couple of weeks ago five men were on the loch and had not a single permit between them. The rain was much heavier now. I was still thinking about my traps. Smiley suggested we should pack up and call it a day, and the bailie volunteered to see us off, but we told him to go on ahead. He set off into the gloom, and that gave us an opportunity to retrieve the traps which we found among the rushes. Setting all six traps and catching no fish was a wee bit disappointing.

Here is my last word on fishing before we get back to coal, well not on fishing exactly, more on style. I noticed that a lot of anglers were wearing denim waistcoats with multi pockets. They looked like walking chests of drawers, which caused me to wonder what an angler takes with him to fill all those pockets. They even wore them in the high street when they weren't fishing. Smiley and Eddie wore them, but I didn't.

"That's why you can't catch fish, you are not dressed properly," Eddie said.

I was hopeful that my thoughtful wife would buy me one, then I too could look like a walking chest of drawers, but I still didn't know what I would put in the pockets.

# CHAPTER FOURTEEN
## RESCUE BRIGADE

I was a member of the Mines Rescue Brigade for ten years as a part time member and became a captain. The Mines Rescue Brigade had permanent teams that were on standby twenty four hours a day, but each colliery, as far as it could, also had a team of trained rescue men on call as part timers. Of course a lot of training was necessary, you had to be fit, and you had to be competent in First Aid. A team consisted of five members and every team had to have completed at least twelve practices in a year. Each member was also subjected, every year, to a fitness test and a medical examination by a doctor.

When part timers were called out to an incident it was generally hours after it had happened, as the full timers were first on the scene. Part timers were called out to allow them to rest. On the job, you were obliged to wear breathing apparatus, which took a bit of getting used to, but during training you were closely watched by the Station Officers.

One incident occurred at a colliery and I was called out. It was not considered life threatening, a spontaneous combustion of waste of a coal face but as a precautionary measure, the workmen were withdrawn from the pit. Just a few were kept down, to assist the rescue teams to build stoppings, which were generally thirty feet in length and were built with sandbags.

These could stop the blast of an explosion, or prevent an explosion from happening. The stoppings were built on the intake and return side of a coal face, in the main gate and tail gate, with the sandbags being filled mostly on the surface and then transported to the site where they were manhandled by the workmen, providing the atmosphere was healthy.

As they were being built, a three by three foot tunnel was left in the middle, thus allowing air to pass through the section to avoid a build up of gas. Should such a build up have occurred, it would have been ignited by the heating, and no one wanted that while working on the site. As you know, all coals emit gas, and thus you have underground explosions, but if you have sufficient air flowing through the workings the gas is diluted and harmless. When I met up with my team at the colliery, we were kitted out with apparatus and sent underground to the site.

We were given the task of watching over the workmen at the stopping, and we had a small oxygen-giving breathing apparatus available which we to give to the workmen, should any of them be overcome by gas. Although we ourselves were wearing breathing apparatus we were not buckled up but the men who had been left down to help build the stoppings didn't like the situation and got a bit stroppy. In the end they were withdrawn to the surface, leaving the stopping building to us, not easy when wearing apparatus.

When both stoppings were completed and the tunnels sealed off, every one was retired to the surface. Before leaving, a telephone was hung next to the main gate stopping with its receiver off the hook. It was connected to the telephone in the Operations Room on the surface and also to a tape recorder which would record the sound of any explosion, should one occur. The pit would be stood down for twenty four hours. It was all a matter of waiting, and we all went home to rest, having been instructed to report back the next day.

The twenty four hours being up with no record of an explosion, the powers that be decided to send down a team to visit the site and report back their findings. Now if the expected explosion hadn't already happened, then it could still happen and the team to be sent down would have to be cautious and alert. Which team did they choose for this dangerous task? Who else but my team? Once again I got the feeling that I was expendable.

We were told to go underground and approach the site from another angle as the direct route was heavily contaminated with C.O. We were to have an escort, a top brass who was not wear breathing apparatus, which suggested to us that he was not going accompany us all the way to the stopping. More than likely, he would just operate the man-rider which would take us down the dook to a level adjacent to the site. A second team would be sent down to the top of the dook, and their task would be to come to our aid should we find ourselves in trouble. We were given a methanometer, but no flame lamp and sample bottles.

Having been briefed by the Station Officer and the Board Officials we were advised to take no risks, and that if things didn't go to our liking we should pull out. I would have pulled out right then and there, but you do what is expected of you. We boarded the man-rider to the bottom of the dook, and it was hauled away from us to the top of the dook. I would have preferred that it stayed at the bottom, but there, that's how it was.

We set off towards the site in single file. I was leading with No 5 coming up in the rear, as usual. We were buckled up and breathing through our apparatus, and went off in the direction of the site. I noticed that the air was a bit hazy, but this was only to be expected, and also warm. We stopped occasionally to take measurements of the atmosphere, and to check each man's oxygen supply. We were in no hurry to get there. With two and a half hours oxygen on our backs and the task only taking an hour, we had ample time. Anyway, wearing apparatus is not the most comfortable way to travel.

Arriving at the site, I examined the stopping and then, while the rest took samples, I made another check of the team's oxygen. I noticed that No. 3's reading was down to less than one hour when the rest of us had almost two hours left. The rule when wearing apparatus is that you must arrive at fresh air with a half hour of oxygen left in your tank.

I was a bit alarmed at this. Could I have misread his dial the first time? Was the dial faulty? Could it be that his oxygen supply was giving off too much oxygen, or maybe there was a leak at the joint? These thoughts were running through my head and I was a bit concerned, not wanting to be caught out in a C.O. atmosphere without oxygen. To go back could be a problem if we encountered a delay. The alternative was to carry on to the tail gate and beyond to fresh air, which we could achieve in under an hour.

I wrote an note on my pad and showed it to No. 5, my deputy; he nodded in agreement. I then sounded 'five' on my hooter to call the team together and showed them the note. They nodded, and we set off towards the tail gate. Earlier I had looked at the main gate stopping and found that, if had there been an explosion, it had no effect at this point. The stopping remained intact, the way we had left it. Arriving at the tail gate we stopped only for a few minutes, just long enough to note that it also remained intact. We then set off on a long haul to fresh air.

We were not to know that earlier, when I had sounded 'five' on my hooter to call the team together, the telephone in the main gate picked up the signal, which was then heard on the surface. For some reason it was not fully understood and, thinking that there might be trouble in our team, the standby team at the top of the dook were immediately telephoned to go and investigate. When they arrived at the first stopping, of course, we weren't there, so they then made their way to the tail gate stopping. When we were not there either, they knew that something was wrong. Knowing that the only other way out was the long way, they went after us in a hurry and eventually caught us up.

On seeing their lights coming towards us, we were a bit surprised, thinking that we were the only team down this far, but getting together all was explained. We were now in fresh air and heading for the nearest telephone where we contacted the surface just in time to avoid a panic.

The surface control room, not knowing what was going on, had alerted the rest of the rescue team to stand by, ready to go underground. That was now called off.

I had a lot of explaining to do at the briefing in the surface control room with them thinking that my actions had been a bit drastic in not turning back in the first instance. That, they reckoned, would have been the right thing to do, but as we were all safe and sound, that was the only thing that mattered.

We never knew if there was an explosion behind the stoppings, but if there was, then the stoppings were solid enough to hold it. However, we did learn later that the C.O. content was very high, and one mouthful of that and you are a goner.

# CHAPTER FIFTEEN

## TRIALS AND TRIBULATIONS

If you ever wondered what it is like to land in court for the first time, especially as a teenager, then read on. In early mining days, as you may have already gathered, all coal underground was transported by haulage rope or hand drawn, which was hard graft, donkey work for the drawer, and when coal was bashing out from the coal face, the young oncost workers were kept going. In an eight hour shift they would only stop for twenty minutes to eat their piece. The young men got hardened to the work but were always tired and glad to see the end of the shift.

The pressure was never lifted, only reinforced by the oversman. He would never let up, was always there in the middle of things, ensuring that there were no hold-ups. He was a big man, tall and strong, was forever dashing here and there like a dog, straining on a lead and attempting to give the impression of a man taking things easy.

He wouldn't even sit down like the rest of us at piece time. Instead, he would be up the coal face to estimate the amount of coal that had to be cleared. The man was always on the move and must have been exhausted by the end of the shift. Our piece time over, he would chase us back to work before he sat down to eat and even then he didn't eat all his bread - a slice or two was always left in his box for whoever wanted it.

At this time I was one of the oncost boys, keeping the empty tub flowing to the loader to be filled. There was virtually an army of us all full of devilment, up to all the tricks, so it was not surprising then that the oversman was forever keeping his eye on us. We all knew that he didn't eat all his piece, and whoever could sneak away first got the bread and came back rubbing his belly and saying, "Boiled ham to day," or "That was great, two lovely slices on roast beef".

Of course, we all knew that it was most likely jam and

margarine. But one day the oversman did not appear for his piece, or at least no one saw him. The cause was a roof fall on the face line and that would probably keep him tied up all day. A fall on the face meant no coal. Everything was at a standstill, with the boys just hung around in groups discussing girls as usual. Of course, the oversman's piece was also on their mind and nobody knew if he had eaten it. The outcome was, one of the boys slipped away and found that the box still had four slices in it. He knew that the owner was still at the face, so decided to take two slices before anyone else got their hands on them and didn't say a word to anyone.

But that wasn't the end of it. Another boy went to the piece box and only seeing two slices, he took them thinking that they had been left for him. Come finishing time, with the oversman still at the face, the boys packed up and went home. When the man returned from the face to find his piece box empty, he thought that maybe his wife had forgotten to make his piece up.

He left it like that until he got home, where his wife rather indignantly assured him that she had indeed made it up. He knew then that the boys had eaten it. Arriving in the section the following morning, where the boys were gathered awaiting the run of coal, he spoke to them.

"In future, no one must touch my piece unless I give them my personal authority, got that?"

As he was speaking he was looking hard at a lad named Waugh. Of course, word had got about that someone had eaten the oversman's piece and it was causing some amusement amongst the boys, especially to Waugh. It was so noticeable that all the boys were all looking at him. He began to feel that he was being accused of the bread swiping. Waugh was a right tearaway amongst the boys and was the most obvious choice, but was entirely innocent. Feeling the glare of the boys on him, he shouted angrily, "What are you looking at me for? I didn't steal your piece."

"If you didn't take it you must know who did,"

"If I knew I wouldn't tell you," bawled Waugh, his face turning red even through the dirt. It was about to develop into a heated argument when a shout from the loader broke up the group.

"The coal's coming."

They all left to get on with their work. For the rest of that day, every time the oversman passed Waugh he would give him a searching look; you know, the kind of look that says 'I'm keeping an eye on you,' which was very unnerving to Waugh and later on, as the oversman passed once more, he shouted, "You want to lay off me, I didn't eat your fucking piece."

The older man, taken aback, said, "You young snipe, no one swears at me and gets away with it."

As he spoke he was leaning over a tub, waving his finger up and down in front of Waugh's nose, with the boys looking on and wondering what was going to happen. Now, this is the important part. According to the boy, he swung his hand up to brush away the oversman's dominating finger and in doing so clipped his chin.

The oversman said that Waugh swung his fist and punched him on the chin. The next instance, the oversman jerked back, causing his helmet to fly off. He was livid, his face was bursting with rage, and we expected him to grab Waugh and give him a good hiding. He just stood there, trying to control his anger, fumbling with his helmet to put it back on his head, and then turned to Waugh.

"Get your jacket on and get up the pit, right now."

We all stood opened mouthed, as none of us had been sacked before and a sacking of a young man was unheard of. All our fathers worked in the pit and our grandfathers before that, and when a young man got out of hand, his own father was told and he would deal with the boy. Waugh was stumped, and in the silence that followed he seemed to be looking for some support from the rest of the boys. He got it, as a voice from the back called out.

"If you send him up the pit then we will all go."

The oversman swung round to find that the voice came from Waugh's brother.

"That's how you all feel then, is it?"

There was silence, with a few nods. The loader-man was calling for empties or otherwise he would have to stop the face conveyor.

"Right," said the oversman, "Everyone back to work and we'll deal with this later." Then he walked away.

Nothing more was said of the incident and we all though that it was over and done with, until the second morning. As I approached the time-office, to collect my token, a head popped out the window. It was the oversman, and he spoke to me asking if I remembered his argument with Waugh the other day. "Of course I do," I replied. "We all do."

I confirmed, thinking nothing of it as I spoke, but then a policeman replaced the oversman at the window and handed me a summons to appear in court. I was shaken, as I had never been in a court before and had no idea what would have to do. All that day at work I didn't mention the summons, and it wasn't till I got home that I told my father.

"Go to court and tell what you saw, just the truth, and it will be alright," was his advice.

He said I would be a witness for the prosecution, against Waugh. Well, that was awful. He palled about with us and lived across the street from me. I couldn't get the court hearing out of my mind. I seemed to be going about in a daze, I had expected some flak from our neighbours and mates, but nobody mentioned anything about the court to me which only made me worse.

The day came when I arrived in court. I was placed in the waiting room and told to wait until I was called, and as I waited, the longer I sat, the more frightened I became. It was as though I was being put on trial, and in a way I was, on trial to tell the truth of the events that happened in the pit.

By the time I was called I was virtually a nervous wreck. Entering the room where the hearing was taking place, being escorted by a court official into a nearly-packed house, I felt that all eyes were on me as I was guided into the witness box.

I looked down on the people in the court house, as the witness box is on a high stand, and everybody was looking back at me. It was terrible, alarming, and I felt trapped. It was then that I saw the judge. He was leaning over his desk staring at me, a big man, red faced with a gown to match and a wig on his head. He frightened me. I prayed never to come up in front of him, if ever I should commit a crime.

*Expendable*

I was sworn in and the judge was telling me to speak up. My face turned red to match the judge's, and I didn't know how my knees were still holding me up. I glanced at the court and recognised some of the men from our pit. They were smiling at me and giving the thumbs up sign. I smiled back feebly and raised my arm to acknowledge their support. In an instant, I realised that I shouldn't have done it, as the judge addressed me in a loud voice.

"Young man, do you realise that you are in a court of law and that this is a serious matter we are dealing with? Now stand up, and answer the questions put to you."

With that he leaned back in his chair and adjusted his gown.

I was glad to get home that day, vowing never to do anything wrong if I had to face up to that judge. The outcome was that Waugh was fined five pounds, and the court official was annoyed that he had to pay out three times that amount to cover our wages and expenses. I was not the only witness for the prosecution, there were three of us.

Although that was my first appearance in a court of law, it was not to be my last, there would be many times in the future when I would have to go to the court, yes have to. I don't think anyone would go to court of their own free will. I also had to make a number of appearances to the Tribunal court, for unfair dismissal cases. One case springs to mind.

A man in his early twenties got dismissed for absenteeism from our pit. He had been given all necessary warnings, which he had ignored, and so, the warnings having no effect on him, he was given notice to terminate his employment. Within a couple of weeks, the pit was notified to attend a tribunal court as the man had claimed unfair dismissal.

I was there to represent the pit as it was part of my duties to deal with absenteeism. No union man was present to represent the man as they had given him up as a lost case and that was what happened. After the evidence was heard the dismissal stood, and he lost his case.

A few weeks later my wife and I were in the local hotel having a few drinks. It was early evening and only a few people were there except a group of men sitting around a table in the corner. They were noisy and loud, which caused us to look in their direction. We were both alarmed to note that one of them was the man that I had dismissed. Obviously, he had spotted me, and he seemed to be pointing me out to the others, or at least that was what I was thinking, so it was then my intention to drink up and get out fast. Before that could happen, our man rose from his table and came towards me. You can imagine what I was thinking.

"My wife doesn't like the sight of blood, especially my blood. I hope someone sends for an ambulance so that I don't have to lie injured on the floor too long."

As it turned out it wasn't like that. He came up to me.

"Hi there," he said, "No hard feelings. As it has turned out you did me a good turn, I've got a better job and more money."

I still drank up and left with my wife. She asked what that had all been about, and when I told her she said, "That could have been nasty,"

"I know, I know," I said, as we walked home. "But I'm wondering how long he will keep his new job."

On another occasion, I found myself in court again on behalf of the pit, or rather the Coal Board, and it proved very interesting, with me putting my foot in it as usual and getting caught in the middle; where the lawyer for the plaintiff bawled me out and my own lawyer, the man meant to be on my side, bawled me out, and even the judge looked at me from under his wig as though I was something that had crawled out from under a stone.

An underground loco driver had delivered a train of empty mine cars from the pit bottom and shunted them behind the loader as was normal. He then drove to the front of the loader to pick up the full train. On his way he was stopped by the loader man, who asked him to give the empties a push, as they were stuck. Our loco driver, in an attempt to push the mine car, received a fractured leg.

He did a silly thing. Instead of going back and getting behind the mine cars to push them forward, he got a four foot wooden strap, set it against the buffer of his loco, with the other end against the side of a mine car and started to push. Of course the strap slipped and struck him on the leg. The loco driver, once he had recovered in hospital, put in a claim for liability against the Board. His claim was based on the fact that he had not been trained to drive the loco, nor been certificated or authorised to drive it. That was where I came in. It was my responsibility to ensure that all workers were trained, qualified and authorised to do the work they were asked to.

Before going to court I received a letter from the board's lawyer asking me to bring to court all the records and certificates in my possession relating to the defendant. So there I was back in the witness box again, the judge looking like the other one, with red face, red gown, white wig, and looking completely bored, as though he was wishing he were somewhere else.

The loco driver's lawyer asked me to tell the court, in detail, of the training I gave to loco drivers. I informed him that I didn't train people, I superintended the training and it was certainly not part of the training to push mine cars with a wooden strap. I knew that I should never have made reference to the strap the minute I said it, as it had never been mentioned up to that time, and I was supposed to answer only to the questions I had been asked.

I looked at the lawyer, and the look on his face was saying, "I'll sort you out before you leave the stand."

I looked at the judge, then at my lawyer, and they both had the same expression on their faces, a holding back smile, the sort of smile you'd expect a terrorist to wear as he watched your execution. I wisely decided to answer all future questions with a yes or no and no speeches.

He then asked. "Is my client authorised to drive the loco?"

"He is," I replied.

"Do you have proof of that and can you produce a copy of authorisation?"

"I can."

"Well, show it to the court if you have it and don't keep us guessing."

I put my hand in my pocket, drew out a certificate and handed it to him. He looked at it, then walked to his client. I saw his client shake his head, and as he returned to me I could see by the smirk on his face that he was thinking, "I told you that I would get you, prepare to be humiliated."

Holding up the piece of paper that I had given him, he said, "Is that my client's signature on this certificate?"

"No." I replied.

"No?" he inquired. He then approached the bench, holding up the certificate like someone who had just found the fiver he'd lost.

"This is not an authorisation for my client to drive a loco, it's a forgery. I suggest that my client was neither trained nor authorised to drive a locomotive and should never have been sent to do so."

With that he put the certificate on the clerk's desk and went back to his chair. Job well done, he must have been thinking. Now I knew that the signature on the certificate was not that of the loco driver because I had printed his name in the place where his signature should be, as I didn't want to be taken up for forgery. I had two copies of the certificate because I had to safeguard the signed copy, and kept the other for reference. It was this reference copy I had handed over.

I was looking to my lawyer for some kind of support, as the judge was sitting up now and taking some interest in the proceedings, looking down his nose at me as if I were a piece of shit. I had managed to upset the previous lawyer and felt hurt by the judge's insinuations. I sure needed a friend but as my lawyer walked up I could see in his face that he was not at all happy either. He looked as if he could shoot me in cold blood. He was livid.

"Did I, or did I not, tell you to bring the authorisation to drive a loco to court with you?" he said.

"You did."

He walked over to the clerk's desk and lifted the certificate, hen turned to me.

"This isn't an authorisation to drive a loco, it's a worthless piece of paper, is it not?"

The judge was nodding in agreement.

"I know," I said.

"You know." he almost shouted. "You know. What then happened to the authentic certificate that I asked you to bring?"

# 158

I put my hand in my pocket and took out the real certificate.

"I have it here," I replied.

The court was in uproar, my lawyer was telling himself he didn't believe what was happening. The other lawyer was on his feet, shouting.

"Objection, Your Honour. They can't produce the certificate now."

The judge filled a glass of water and drank it down in one swallow. An argument followed, with both lawyers glowering at me. The judge hadn't changed his mind. I was still a piece of shit in his eyes. I was glad to get home.

# CHAPTER SIXTEEN
## TRAVEL TOURS UNDERGROUND

You may not believe me when I tell you that underground can be the safest place to be in the world. Ask any old miner. Of course, there can be explosions, huge falls of roof, inrushes of water and poisonous gases to mention but a few, but there are some places underground which are absolutely safe. It's curious, that with most pits there are always visitors wishing to go underground, M.Ps, Ministers of the church, local business men, school parties, and even miners' wives. My wife has been down a number of pits. She says it's awful, but that's where our livelihood comes from. It was part of my job to escort visitors under ground and I preferred an inquisitive group, people who were nosy and wanted to ask questions; they were always welcomed.

But not all parties are of that category. Some, the minute they step off the cage, want to go back up to the surface, while others remain silent, ask no questions and finish the visit without a word, until they get to the surface and then you can't keep them quiet. I prefer the inquisitive type, very keen, very interested but they can ask you some embarrassing questions.

"Where do you keep the toilets underground?" is one example.

"Miners have learnt to regulate their bowels and don't require toilets underground," I would reply. "But surely there must be times when they are caught out?"

"Yes there are times, and in these instances the toilet is under a flat stone in the waste or old road."

It had to be remembered that visitors, if they hadn't been under ground before, were a bit apprehensive, nervous, and where the walking track is not ideal for walking, nor at times is the roof high enough to stand up, so they would stumble and fall and try as they might to walk in a stooping posture, virtually doubled up, they would continually bump their head on the roof and fall back on their end. I started this story telling you about the nice and comfortable

*Expendable*

place that underground can be, and so I will. Generally, on the later part of a visit, when the visitors are feeling a bit tired and sore from their ordeal, I take them to an old roadway that has long been worked out, where the roof has settled, and it is nice and warm. I get them to sit on the floor with their legs stretched out in front, and backs resting against the side of the roadway, and relax. When they are settled, I tell them then that if they ever wanted to find out what it was like to be dead, they are about to know.

They are told not to make a sound, be still and relax, and then to put their lights out. The place immediately falls into total blackness, a darkness so thick that it can be felt, you actually feel that you can grab handfuls. You can hear your visitors take a sharp intake of breath, then all is quiet again. The only sound to be heard is of your own heart beating, and even that quietens and then you hear nothing. They lose their senses, can't see, can't hear and can't feel. Then after a few moments I speak to them in a low voice from the darkness and tell them it's wonderful, absolute peace, there is no war down here, no television, no radio, nothing to distract them, and to enjoy the moment, because for the rest of their lives they may never find this peace of mind again.

You know I used to think we were on to a good thing here and wondered if a travel agent would be interested? Think of it - "Four days underground, £250 a head. You'll never be the same again. Menu : two on jam, two on cheese, and water."

Every job, I suppose, has its compensation, that is, to feel within one's self that one is doing something worth while, with the reward of job satisfaction and contentment. I got my contentment from visiting the local school and talking to the children. It all came about from a request by the head teacher of the local school, who apparently, seemed a bit concerned that the children were crossing our railway line to play in the fields beyond. The head teacher asked for someone from the pit to come and tell the children of the dangers associated with living close to a colliery and of the things that should be avoided.

The first visit was a great success, and I based future such visits on that first one. I would start off such a visit by talking about mines and miners in general, not the heavy stuff, but enough to get the children interested. After all, their fathers and brothers would probably work in the mine and when they grew up they'd be miners too, I supposed. I would have miners' helmets, lamps and knee pads with me and would dress up a couple of boys with this gear. Then I would upend three or four chairs and get the boys to crawl through and under the chairs, with the class room lights out. The kids loved this, if their laughter was any thing to go on.

I would also take the pit's projector with me and show a I would also take the pit's projector with me and show a cartoon to settle them before going on to talk about the dangerous side of all this. I would explain that they knew not to touch wet paint, just to see if it really was wet, nor touch a pot on the stove, to see if it was hot, but did they always do what they were told to do, or not to do? I would give them a little demonstration of what could happen to a person who did not do as he or she was told, but did, instead, what he or she thought was right. I would take with me a piece of hardboard four feet long by two and a half feet wide, which I'd place on the floor. Requesting the assistance of two boys, I would get them to stand, one at the front and one at the back, lift the board and take one pace forward and stop. Whilst the two boys were standing there I would then tell them a true story, which went like this:

"Two men were sent to the stores compound, to ask the storekeeper for a metal plate, just the same size as the one you boys are holding. Off they went and as they entered the compound there, on the floor, to their delight, was a metal plate, just the size they were looking for, lying right in the middle of the path. They didn't go to the storekeeper as they were told, but instead decided to take the plate which was handy, and picking it up between them they started to walk away with it."

Then I would take away the boy behind the board, leaving the boy in front holding the board on his own. The class would be very attentive, looking on, waiting.

"What do you think happened? " I asked, "The man at the back has disappeared. Where has he gone?"

*Expendable*

They would look puzzled, until I told them that he had fallen down a hole, the hole that the plate was covering. They all thought that it was so funny; hilarious, and I would then try again to be more serious. I would spend the rest of the time talking about the dangers of playing near, or on, the railway and would finish up by asking them to take part in a competition, by drawing our train and railway.

That first visit was just the beginning; it snowballed from there and soon virtually all the schools in the surrounding area wanted a talk from us. Even the local Round Table asked for one.

Smiley agreed to allow a visit from our local school. It was arranged for them to go underground and I was to take them along the main level to the man rider, down the dook and on to the coal face, but not to take them actually on to the face.

The kids arrived and were met in the yard and taken to the conference room to be kitted up. Twenty-one kids came, with three teachers and that allowed us to take Eddie and the V.O., so that the party could be split up into three groups. With a final warning from Smiley we set off, I with my party coming up in the rear. The teachers, all female, confessed that they had never been underground before and while being lowered down the shaft they closed their eyes and bravely held onto the kids who were too small to reach the handrail. Getting off the cage at the pit bottom, they stood and looked about.

"Where's the coal?" they asked, as if expecting to see miners digging coal right at the bottom of the shaft. Eddie explained that it was about two miles away. It was all explained to them as we walked the travelling road, where no locos or transport were running, to the top of the dook and the man-rider. We had travelled only three quarters of a mile and it had taken the best part of an hour.

The kids were looking up at the roof most of the time and not watching were they put their feet, so they were liable to stumble, but fortunately nobody did. There were a number of girls in the party - they stuck closely together near their teacher while the boys walked on in front and had to be continually called back. They all had trouble with their helmets, which were too big and kept falling over their eyes and we had to stop and make a number of adjustments.

*Expendable*

The man-rider was waiting for us and we all climbed aboard. The seats being so very close to each other meant that the person sitting opposite would have to spread their knees to allow your knees to fit in between theirs, and that's where I could have swallowed my tongue. As I climbed on board, a teacher was sitting opposite to me and I, innocently, honest, said, "Would you mind opening your legs and let me in."

She understood what I meant and, quite unconcerned, answered, "My, that's the best offer I've had all day."

As for me, you could have lit a fag off my face. Reaching the bottom and climbing out of the man-rider, we crossed into the main gate where the conveyor was loading out the coal. We stopped every few minutes to answer questions. It was warm and moist, the damp air causing fungus to grow from the timbers like white balls of cotton wool. I began telling them that underground there is no colour, and asking them if they knew the reason. They didn't and so, getting into this teaching lark, I told them that there is no colour underground because there is no sun, and it's sunshine that gives colours. One little girl pointed to her jersey, which was red, and asked, "Why is it still red then?"

"It was red before it came down here and it will always be red where there's light," I explained.

There was silence, then the teacher pointed out, "Surely, everything that is down here has been brought down from the surface with its colour?"

By then, I was changing my mind about being a teacher, and I was not going to be dragged into a biology discussion; because that's where it was leading.

"Perhaps I should give a better example," I said. "Take the fungus, it's never seen daylight."

I quickly changed the subject by pointing to the coal on the conveyor because I knew that the next question to be thrown at me would be about where the fungus came from. I suggested to the kids that they take a piece of coal from the side of the roadway where the coal had not been excavated, and told them that they would be the first person to touch that piece of coal since the world began. It took a trick with them and they happily put a piece of coal into their pocket with the teacher saying that she had never looked at it in that way before and she also took a bit of coal. When we eventually returned to the surface, three hours later, the conference room was laid out for the kids with tea, sandwiches and biscuits. We were glad to get them all safely up to the surface and by the noise in the conference room I think they had enjoyed their visit.

# CHAPTER SEVENTEEN

## FINALE

In spite of, or maybe because of the dreadful conditions, there was a lot of humour and comradeship in the mines. It was a man's world, just like the army, all men together, working closely with each other, depending on each other, all to the same goal. The army has its corporals and sergeants to give orders, the pit had deputies and oversmen to do the same thing and men lose their lives in both outfits.

When men share such a life of comradeship, practical jokes are never far away. Anyone who caused offence down the mines was often repaid in this way. The wood boys had one day been unable to find their homer, a piece of wood cut off the end of a tree and used as a support.

The hole borer had previously asked the wood boys to cut a homer for him and they had refused and so he became the prime suspect. The boys believed he had taken it home to kindle the house fire. To teach him a lesson, they cut a homer with a large knot in it, pushed it up into the sleeve of the hole borer's jacket and nailed it in. The hole borer went home that day with one sleeve hanging loose on his jacket wondering who could have done this. He believed that it was the pumper, with whom he sat at piece time, because although they sat together, they would argue a lot. With that on his mind, he wanted revenge, and when the opportunity arose he nailed the pumper's piece box to the wooden seat and said nothing.

Now it was the pumper's turn to get mad, and he'd gone home without his piece box. He knew that only one person could have done it and he felt that he had to even things up. The next day the hole borer was boring a hole for a stripper when they both experienced a nasty smell and kept looking at each other, suggesting that might be where the smell was coming from but, as the hole was being bored and the threads of the screw were advancing, out from the barrel of the borer excrement was oozing, where it should have

*Expendable*

been grease. The pumper had got his revenge by putting it into the barrel of the borer. After all that, it turned out to be the gaffer who was pinching the homers.

Miners got themselves involved in all kinds of dodges even, I was told, my own father. He, like most miners, would skin from his wages before he gave them to his wife and many a tall tale and often an ingenious plan was brought into operation in order to skin a few bob. My father's plan, if I can recall, was a straightforward 'money in hand' plot, which was told to me much later by mother.

It was like this. Father had a contract going, down in the local mine, and claimed that he had been paid short over a period of weeks. He won his claim and got the back-money which nobody, not even my mother, knew anything about. The extra money amounted to a gold sovereign. Arriving home, telling my mother that his wages were in his pocket, and not letting on that the sovereign was in his hand, which was tightly closed, he removed his pit clothes and got ready to wash. Still with the sovereign in his hand he picked up the soap, a half bar of carbolic, into which, to his relief, he was able to push the sovereign. Washed, cleaned-up and dressed, he was ready to go for a pint, but there was no sign of the carbolic.

"Where is the soap?" he asked.

"I borrowed it from the next door and just gave it back," said Mum.

Humour is important to miners and they are happy to take a joke against themselves. You have probably heard this story before. The Police in London were clamping down on prostitutes in an attempt to drive them off the streets. A Member of Parliament said that the police tactics would only drive the prostitutes underground.

"Lucky miners," exclaimed another member, "they get everything that is going."

Another story tells of miners at a pit who went on strike and the manager inquired why.

"It's the dust, we can't see our hand in front of our face for it." replied the miners.

The manager, a well educated type, told them that the dust they see wouldn't do them any harm, and that it was the dust they couldn't see that they should worry about. However, he did install a water system to keep the dust down and the men went back to work. But it was not for long before they were back up the pit again.

"What's the matter this time?" asked the manager.

"Well," the men said, "remember you told us that it was the dust you can't see that is harmful"

"Yes," said the manager.

"Well, the place is full of it."

The pits were eventually closed and the work force made redundant. I was over sixty years of age at the time and accepted the situation but after a few months of rising in the morning with nothing laid on for me to do, just flitter about, look out the window to see if the rain had stopped, drink a lot of tea, walk sometimes, and be left with a lot of memories I looked for something to do and decided to pass those memories on to you.

Like a good wine, I have deliberately kept the love of my life to the end of the story, a love that has been with me throughout most of my life. A love, which I could not hope to obtain, I was allowed only to gaze at and admire. Of all God's creatures, to me this was his greatest gift to mankind, a gift to remind man that he is mortal. A mystery, which he allowed us to know, bit by bit, but will never let us reach the end, because there is no ending to knowledge. The love of my life then, apart from the wife of course, is astronomy.

Even before I left school, like everyone else I suppose, I could look up to the sky on a summer's night and marvel at the millions of twinkling diamonds that god had installed. Even when still young, I could recognise the Seven Sisters, the North Star and the Plough as we knew it, yet no one ever seemed to take it seriously or a step nearer; it was left to us, in our child's minds, to make some sense of this array. I imagined a huge globe circulating the earth with all the stars stuck on to it. Perhaps I got the idea from our church, whose dome above the altar was decorated in stars. Then it was a topic of the day, and we would just look up and wonder.

It wasn't until I returned from the R.A.F. that my thoughts began to dwell on astronomy, again in a very amateur way. With the Americans and Russians putting rockets into orbit and landing men

*Expendable*

on the moon, you just had to sit up and take notice. Astronomy has come a long way in the last forty years and now nearly everybody on our planet knows something about our solar system

I still have a great passion to learn of the latest discoveries, and acquired a telescope, a four and a half inch, which I used frequently to look into the night sky.

I wrote earlier about the joy of coming up the pit at the end of a shift with the sun reaching down into the shaft. In the morning, after a night shift, it was the stars that welcomed us safely back to the surface.

No-one who hasn't experienced it can imagine the contrast between the blackness of the pit, hidden from sun moon and stars, and the universe above. Man can only look at the heavens with wonder and speculate.

I spent forty six years of my life like a mole, tunnelling underground. Maybe it is not too surprising, then, that now I look to the stars.

# GLOSSARY

AFC ...armoured face conveyor
Blaes...blue stone, clay
Brushing...enlargement of the roadway at the face
CCEE...Colliery Chief Electrical Engineer
CCME...Colliery Chief mechanical Engineer
C.O... carbon monoxide
COSA...Colliery Staff Association
Chock wood...square cut 4in x 4in x 3ftfor pillar building as roof support
Close was near... roof about to cave in
Coal cutting machine... a low 16ft machine with a toothed jib which picks or undercuts the coal to a depth of four feet
Coalface... up to 200 yards long where coal is extracted
Cuttings...chippings from the coal cutter
Doddle...easy
Deputy... official responsible to the manager in matters of safety and working operations
Development and stone mining... driving roadways to reach the coal
Dook – mining workings below the level of the pit bottom
Filling and drawing... a stripper, with no access to a conveyor, will shovel his coal behind him; the filler will shovel the coal into a hutch and when it's full take it away and bring back an empty one
Graith...tools such as pick, shovel, hammer, etc.
Half a spat of ajax...3 ounces of explosives
Homer...a piece of wood for fire kindling
Jigger pans... 10 ft long pans, all bolted together to form a chute-like conveyor, covering the entire length of the coal face
Lousing ...end of shift
Low side... road head and main gate where coal has not been removed
Main gate...main roadway to the coal face
Metals...rocks
Methanometer...gas detector

*Expendable*

NACODS...National Association of Colliery Overmen, Deputies and Shotfirers
NUM National Mineworkers Union
Oncost...transport worker
Pack... dry stone dyke, infilled with rubbish, that acts as a roof support
Pan engine...a machine with a long arm attached to the pans which jigs them forward
Piece...snack
Pit bings...slag heaps
Pit bottomer...man in charge at the bottom of the shaft
Props or trees...wooden upright supports
Pumper...the man who is in charge of the water pumps
Redd...waste
Road head... the end of the main gate at the bottom of the run
Roof close...roof cave in
Run or face... coal face
SCEBTA...Scottish Colliery Enginemen, Boilermen and Tradesmen Association
Sharok alarm...explosive magazine alarm
Shearer...coal cutter and loader
Shears... one shear of coal advances 3 feet
Shot...a hole charged with explosive and fire
Skip wind...coal brought up in a skip or container instead of a cage. It works automatically, no manpower needed
Square work...girders built as goalposts
Stile or staill...a support set at 45 degrees to prevent an object from falling over
Straps...2in x4in x4ft plank of wood set to the roof and secured by props and trees
Stripper...coal face worker
Top end or tail gate...exit from the coal face, which allows air to circulate
Waste...the area left behind as the coal face advances
Waste tight... the roof down solid on the floor
Wood pillar... wooden straps, built in a pillar as a roof support